AF527865

Dalit Leadership in Panchayats

Dalit Leadership in Panchayats

A Comparative Study of Four States

NARENDER KUMAR
MANOJ RAI

INDIAN INSTITUTE OF DALIT STUDIES, NEW DELHI

RAWAT PUBLICATIONS
Jaipur • New Delhi • Bangalore • Mumbai • Hyderabad

ISBN 81-316-0028-9
© Indian Institute of Dalit Studies, 2006

Published in association with
Indian Institute of Dalit Studies
D/25-D, South Extension, Part II, New Delhi 110 049
Phone: 011-51643981/82 Fax: 011-51643982
E-mail: iids@dalitstudies.org
Website: www.dalitstudies.org

No part of this book may be reproduced or transmitted in any form or by any means, electronic or mechanical, including photocopying, recording or by any information storage and retrieval system, without permission in writing from the publishers.

Published by
Prem Rawat for **Rawat Publications**
Satyam Apts., Sector 3, Jawahar Nagar, Jaipur 302 004 (India)
Phone: 0141 265 1748 / 7006 Fax: 0141 265 1748
E-mail: info@rawatbooks.com
Website: www.rawatbooks.com

New Delhi Office
4858/24, Ansari Road, Daryaganj, New Delhi 110 002
Phone: 011-23263290

Also at Bangalore, Mumbai and Hyderabad

Typeset by Rawat Computers, Jaipur
Printed at Chaman Enterprises, New Delhi

Contents

Preface

Dalits form a major chunk of Indian population. In general, Dalits are socially, economically, educationally and politically deprived. Most of them do not have access to enough food, health care, housing or clothing. Their lives lag behind on all objective indicators of socio-economic development. Untouchability, though a legal crime, still has its presence in social practices. Caste and patriarchy are two major evils of Indian social system, which have yet not disappeared in 'independent' India.

Knowing entrenched caste system in villages, it would have been almost impossible to imagine that there will come a day when our villages will be headed by Dalit man or woman. But it is a reality now. The 73rd Constitutional Amendment Act, 1992 has provided legal sanction to reservation of seats for women and Dalits for the posts of heads and members in panchayats. New constitutional democratic panchayat system has provided legal legitimacy to Dalit leadership. There are more than half million men and women from scheduled castes who have contested and won panchayat elections to occupy political spaces at local levels.

But legal orders are challenged by existing social orders of casteism and patriarchy. Legal orders may be necessary but certainly not sufficient measures to build Dalit leadership at local levels. Most of the Dalit leaders in panchayats are first timers, illiterate and economically dependent on higher castes. Their political inexperience, coupled with constraining casteist social system, is one of greatest inhibiting factors in exercising their leadership at local levels.

What have been experiences so far of Dalit leaders in panchayats? How do they perceive their new-found roles? What are enabling and inhibiting factors? What changes these affirmative actions (of Constitution) have brought out at ground levels? What needs to be done to make Dalit leadership more effective so that it brings out positive changes in qualities of lives of its people? These are some of the questions which need to be addressed.

Though, PRIA in collaboration with 14 universities in 12 states of India launched a national study to develop an understanding of the prospects, constraints and the support structures of Dalits as they grapple to fit into political roles but here only six studies conducted in four states have been selected. Interestingly, though situations in different states vary, there are certain factors, which are common across the states. Education, experience, family, community, economic independence and personal initiatives have been found to be enabling factors for effectiveness of Dalit leadership. Caste practices are most important inhibiting factor in all states. But studies recognize the potential of Dalit leadership in panchayats. These local leaders have capacities to bring those irreversible positive changes in our social system, which could not be achieved by democratically elected state and union governments.

The present book is an effort to make the findings of these studies known to larger audience. We are happy that Narender Kumar of IIDS with the able guidance of Prof. Sudha Pai, has put the data together and analysed them to give the study an academic orientation. Manoj Rai of PRIA with Priyanka Dale have put activistic inputs and have made this publication a joint venture of both the institutions. Finally, we would like to thank all the researchers and participants of national study on Dalit Leadership in Panchayats without whose efforts it would not have been possible to pen down this book.

Sukhadeo Thorat
Rajesh Tandon

Acknowledgements

This book is based on the data collected by various institutions in the country on the initiation of Participatory Research in Asia (PRIA) to look into the emerging pattern of Dalit leadership in panchayats in various states of India. It was the academic interest of the Indian Institute of Dalit Studies (IIDS) and particularly of its Director, Prof. Sukhadeo Thorat that made the data collected to be utilised and bring it out in a book form. Though, many a time, situation arose where I felt disturbed after looking into the incomparable and uneven data collected by various individuals but he came out with one or the other solution. So I am thankful to Prof. Thorat for not only showing confidence in me to bring out this book but also for his valuable suggestions.

A number of persons helped me in this attempt. The first one who immediately comes to mind is Prof. Sudha Pai, Centre for Political Studies, Jawaharlal Nehru University. She has been associated with this project from the very beginning and while finalising the formulations, she provided immense help so that the haphazard data could make academic sense. I feel indebted to her.

Mr. Manoj Rai of PRIA, who is co-author of the book, has always been helpful and also suggested to give academic-activistic orientation to the book. Dr. Umakant of NCDHR, who earlier was with IIDS, needs special mention as he initially accepted the project.

My partner Anju has always been encouraging to complete the work. I feel grateful to her also for caring our small daughter Gautami so that she does not disturb me during work.

Thanks to Mr. Narendra of IIDS for scanning and typing the relevant data for the book.

A few other friends and well-wishers like Rajasekhar Vundru, Ravi Patil, Y.S. Alone, etc., have also been inspiring in this endeavour.

Narender Kumar

1

Introduction

Dalit Leadership in the New Panchayats

The granting of reservations to Dalits[1] within the new panchayats established by the 73rd Constitutional Amendment Act in 1993 is one of the most significant changes introduced in recent decades. Apart from seats for Dalits in every panchayat based on their population, the post of Sarpanch together with one-third of the seats for Dalit women have been reserved. These provisions have the potential of throwing up a new leadership among Dalits who can play a seminal role in participation and decision-making in the new panchayats. Moreover, the amendment has given panchayats constitutional status making them a third tier within the federal structure. Other institutional anomalies which existed in the past have been removed: elections have to be held regularly, the powers and responsibilities of panchayats have been increased and clearly defined and state finance commissions established to provide adequate finances. Panchayats have emerged as an important level within the federal structure, play a more determining role in state politics and have the capacity to carry out development at the local level. Thus, reservation at the panchayat level is today a more important avenue of political participation for

Dalits than within central and state legislatures. It has opened the doors of the political arena for emergent Dalit leaders to enter democratic politics and introduce change at the local level.

Traditionally, leadership in the village was confined to 'rural elites' who were, generally speaking, aged and moderately educated, belonging to the higher castes with links to state political leaders and the bureaucracy (Chakraborty and Bhattacharyya, 1993). A principal characteristic of this elite was landownership, which was not only the main source of subsistence at the village level but was also crucial in determining the rural stratification system and the power structure (Beteille, 1974). It created dependency of the landless lower caste workers on the higher landowning castes. The traditional caste hierarchy placed the Dalit at the bottom and also bred habits of deference of the lower caste to the higher caste, of the younger to the aged, unquestioning obedience of the landless agricultural workers to the landlord, and subservience of the poor to the wealthy. These features 'legitimized' the exercise of power by the powerful landowning and wealthy higher caste section of the village. The village authority structure worked in the form of rule, domination, influence, control, or even in its ugly form and naked manifestation of use of brute force or physical coercion by this group. Studies also point to factions within villages, which were often led by the upper castes and had followers from among the lower castes. Factional leaders, thus, controlled villages and politics within them (Chakraborty and Bhattacharyya, 1993).

A number of village studies beginning in the 1960s by sociologists described this structure, though they did point to new forces in the post-independence period which were beginning to produce economic and political systems that no longer depended entirely on caste. Newer forms of domination in which caste and class forces came together were noted in which power remained in the hands of the higher castes and oppression of the lower castes continued (Beteille, 1974; Srinivas, 1960).

In this setting, rapid social change produced in the rural areas brought a group to whom Beteille described as the 'ambidextrous class' which pointed to the coexistence and interpenetration of two different sets of values with implications for local institutions (Beteille, 1974:106). These were leaders who were able to easily handle both bureaucratic procedures and personal contacts to settle disputes, get things done and have influence over others. Their authority was sanctioned by the traditional caste structure as they belonged to the higher castes. The leader was able to do these things because of the respect he commanded or because of the power he wielded over the villagers. What we find is the coexistence of two kinds of social systems each having its own characteristic mode of organization and norms. The first was organized in terms of caste, kinship and community relationships with a high value placed on personal loyalties and ties of personal dependence. While the second was the organizational nexus or the 'office' where relations are in principle governed by impersonal values and standards (ibid). In India, as villages were, and still remain, characterized by ties of caste and kinship, these two intersect and reinforce each other. Leaders were expected to help their caste brethren and to exercise power on their behalf.

These vertical relationships are undergoing change and it would be more difficult for upper caste leaders today to control the village authority structure and expect subservience from the lower castes. Exercise of power is no longer hereditary, given, automatic and unchallenged. With the introduction of democracy, universal adult franchise and democratic decentralization through the PRIs (Panchayati Raj Institutions), the base of power and its exercise have notably undergone change. New sources and forms of power have emerged, though at the same time the older sources and forms have not disappeared. Leadership is closely connected to and cannot be understood apart from these changes taking place in society. It can no longer be studied under the dominant-dependent paradigm. Scholars point to three stages – traditional, transitional and democratic. In the traditional stage it is quite natural that the political structure will be oligarchic and the dominant caste will rule and common villagers and lower castes will have practically no access to power positions. In the second stage, certain ambivalences appear and traditional ascriptive identities tend to get weakened in the face of achievements of education and wealth. But ruling autocratic forces still remain in control. This is a phase of both democratic and aristocratic politics. This is followed by the democratic stage where caste as a basic feature continues to be important, but loses its traditional legitimizing role and becomes one variable among many. Scholars have argued that in India this process is underway but is at different levels in different areas rendering the process very complex (Shiviah et al., 1978: 122-23).

The new panchayats are now a decade old and in almost all states two elections have been held since the passage of the Act. In terms of sheer numbers, the large number of elected representatives represent a substantial change in the composition of panchayats. This study examines with the use of empirical materials, whether reservations provided by the 73rd Amendment Act has enabled the rise of a new leadership among Dalits, including Dalit women, who as Sarpanchas and Panchas have been able to take advantage of this provision and play a meaningful role through participation and decision-making in the newly constituted panchayats. It analyzes the extent to which they have been able to introduce more *democratic* and *inclusive* patterns of participation and development at the local level. The larger theoretical issue addressed is *the efficacy of reservation as an instrument of socio-political change in a democratic society*.

Second, based on the field studies, the study identifies the enabling/disabling factors that have enabled or hindered Dalits from functioning as effective leaders of panchayats. What are the *socio-economic factors* in specific contexts – states, regions, districts – which provide a setting in which reservations can play a more meaningful role. Why is there a differential impact; why is there hostility and antagonism in some places and acceptance of reservations by the "upper/middle castes" in others? What is the impact of education, social movements, faster economic development and competition arising from it on reservations? Or, these enabling/disabling factors could be located in the *institutional mechanisms* of representation, reservation and participation provided to Dalits and women at the panchayat level.

Third, the study goes beyond identifying the enabling/disabling factors, and it discusses the need for corrective measures and makes specific policy suggestions to overcome the constraints identified, such as electoral innovations, regulatory mechanisms, third party monitoring (by the bureaucracy) for the panchayats. It also discusses what the government, NGOs and bureaucracy can do to overcome the constraints faced by Dalit leadership.

The significance of our study on leadership in the new panchayats must be understood within a larger perspective. The passing of the 73rd amendment has coincided with a number of changes that have taken place both within the Dalit community and in the Indian society and polity. The 1980s witnessed an acceleration of the long-term processes of democratization and regionalization experienced by the Indian society and polity in the Republican period. A number of scholars have pointed out that the power of the rural elite has been questioned though not broken. Writing in the early 1990s Mendelsohn pointed out that with economic development, education and emergence of new forms of non-agricultural employment, land is no longer the only source of power and prestige in rural India (Mendelsohn, 1993: 804-42). In a similar vein, a more recent study of western UP shows that the traditional structures of rural dominance based upon land and social status are undergoing change due to education, diversification of the occupational structure, and government welfare/

development programmes leading to new caste/class equations emerging in the countryside between the traditionally dominant landowning castes and the Dalits (Pai, 2002). A second challenge to the rural elite has come from the rise of political consciousness among the lower castes leading to an upsurge from below questioning the traditional caste hierarchy. This has taken the shape of socio-political mobilization, construction of identity, rise in the number of Dalits voting and emergence of parties led by Dalits and associations (Pushpendra, 2001; Pai, 2002; Pai and Singh, 1997; Lieten and Srivastava, 1999).

These shifts have been matched by corresponding changes within the Dalit community. Literacy rates among the Dalits rose faster during the 1980s. They had increased by only a little over 4 per cent between 1971 and 1981 but between 1981 and 1991 the increase was 8 per cent – a little over 7 per cent among men and 5 per cent among women. Despite the fact that literacy rates and the educational attainments of Dalits are still abysmally low in parts of the country, this is the area in which some change has occurred since the 1970s. School enrolment rates also rose during this decade. There were also reports of improvement in the economic conditions of Dalits in some parts of the country providing them with the potential to revolt against ill-treatment by the higher castes. For example, in UP, studies point to improvements in the socio-economic conditions of Dalits from the late 1970s. In eastern UP, the Green Revolution leading to increase in investment in agriculture and urbanization, increased employment opportunities on farms, brick kilns, construction activities, and rickshaw pulling in cities, removing the absolute dependence on landowners and patron-client relations (Shankar, 1993). In the Western plains, where the condition of Dalits was already better off, a significant shift has been a movement away from land to other sources of livelihood. Due to spread of education, a small urban professional and entrepreneurial elite has arisen which has made use of job quotas to shift to non-agricultural employment (ibid).

Voting percentages among Dalits have also risen and faster than in the general population. In many areas Dalits have voted for the first time since independence. The spread of the power of the vote has been a very important means of raising confidence to revolt against 'upper caste' domination. In the 1996 elections, the percentage of Dalit voter turnout at the national level was 87.3 per cent, the corresponding figure for the upper castes being 85.6 per cent. In the 1998 elections the Dalit voter turnout rose to 93 per cent and the national average to 91.9 per cent. These figures assume significance when we realize that Dalit voter turnout in 1971 was 78.7 per cent (Pushpendra, 1999: 2611).[2] In short, by the 1990s many scholars pointed to the rise of a new republican, educated, upwardly mobile generation among the Dalits with higher levels of consciousness of identity and who were not prepared to put up with domination and oppression.[3] However, these changes have taken place only in a few parts of the country, the pace of change has been slow and poverty remains. Second, only a small section among the Dalits in each region has benefited from these developments, while the large mass of the Dalits due to their disadvantaged position could not benefit from them. Moreover, such social and political changes may not make themselves felt immediately at the panchayat level. It is more difficult for Dalit leaders to assert themselves and introduce change at the *village* than at the national or state or even the district level. This is because it is at the village level that the greatest oppression is experienced by Dalits and the village panchayats are the most vulnerable.

Another significant aspect is that the need for inclusion of Dalits is even greater today. The constitutionalization of the panchayats has meant establishment of three tiers of federalism and greater powers and responsibilities – financial and developmental – in the hands of these institutions. With the introduction of economic reforms at the state level in the mid-nineties, there has been an increasing recognition among scholars and policy makers that poor-oriented programmes – employment, basic social services, PDS, social security – are best implemented in a decentralized manner by PRIs with community participation and subject to local accountability (Guhan, 1995: 248). This view gained ground due to the failure of many state governments, especially those in the backward states of the northern belt, to meet the basic needs of their citizens, particularly the disadvantaged sections. In order to introduce these changes, greater devolution of powers to PRIs, removal of corruption and inefficiency, and higher levels of accountability and participation were needed. The passage of the 73rd Constitutional Amendment in 1993 had already made devolution of power to panchayats part of the agenda of all state governments. Thus, economic reforms and reform of the functioning of panchayats came to be seen as complementary.[4] In this scenario, the participation of Dalits in the functioning of PRIs has become important to ensure that they are included in vital decisions affecting development in the rural areas.

Panchayats: A Brief Historical Sketch

Historical development of PRIs can be studied under two different headings, i.e., pre-independence era and post-independence era.

Pre-Independence Era

Village in Indian history has always been an important socio-economic unit. From the time immemorial, India has a systematic procedure of governing, when these villages were self-dependent and self-sustaining. The little panchayats were flourishing which were autonomous of external pressures. But it was only up till 10th century that these institutions had some developmental phase. After the advent of Mughal rule the external pressures from emperors' side increased thus interfering in working of republican governments of these small units. The introduction of systems like 'jagir' weakened the powers of village panchayats. The inclusion of intermediaries for collecting revenue hampered the growth of self-governing institutions. By the time the British held political power in India, the traditional system of governance was almost non-existent.

In 1915, a resolution was passed to constitute local self-government by provincial governments in selected areas on experimental basis. It further recommended to empower panchayats with the power to levy taxes. Some other recommendations were also made but this resolution did not come into effect. Then came the Government of India Resolution of 1918 in which emphasis was made to legislate to accelerate the rate of progress of the village population. It recommended that separate legislation should be made other than municipal and rural boards. Thus, the British Parliament passed an Act, i.e., Government of India Act, 1919, under which local self-government was made one of the provincial transferred subjects under the charge of a popular minister. Following this, many Acts were passed for the establishment of village panchayats right from 1919 till 1925 and many others till the attainment of independence but all these were on papers only, as the provinces did not want to part with their powers.

In 1935, the Government of India Act, 1935 was passed by the British Government. When popular ministries assumed offices in 1937, they undertook legislation to make local bodies truly representatives (Majumdar and Singh, 1997: 65). But, once again, the whole system turned upside down when the Second World War broke out and for a certain period it was Governor's autocracy that was prevailing. Thus, village panchayats felt completely neglected during this period. Till pre-independence period, the local self-governments were not truly representative and no legal powers were assigned to them. Still, the format laid down by British was very helpful in giving shape to Panchayati Raj in India.

During the Constitution-making, in 1948, a meeting of ministers of local self-government in provinces was held under the chairmanship of Jawaharlal Nehru in which he insisted that local self-government is, and must be, the basis of any true system of democracy. On 22nd November, 1948, K. Santhanam moved a motion in which proposal of organizing village panchayats by states was forwarded which was unanimously adopted.

Since then, the organization of panchayats became an inseparable part of the Constitution that was incorporated its Article 40, which says that "the state shall take steps to organize village panchayats and endow them with such powers and authority as may be necessary to enable them to function as unit of self-government".

The word 'self-government' has been used in the Constitution giving it a prominent position but it was not obligatory for the states as it was included in the Directive Principles of State Policy. However, the developments that took place in the pre-independence period and framing of Indian Constitution gave recognition to Panchayati Raj framework but due to lack of effective implementation policies, it did not assume a place of priority and its roots still remained weak giving a setback to the proper development of this institution.

Post-Independence Era

In post-independence era, Panchayati Raj assumed greater significance as most of the population was residing in villages and the utmost importance lied in making people participate in affairs of the state. The first systematized Community Development Programme (CDP) started in 1952 with the help of USA.

The central objective of CDP was to make people participate in the developmental process. The Block Development Officers, alongwith Gram Sevaks and Sevikas, were appointed to guide as well as persuade people to participate in the government's programmes. But various factors like lack of consciousness, finances, proper leadership etc. made the success of these programmes very limited.

It was Balwantrai Mehta Committee which was appointed in 1956 to assess as to how far CDP has succeeded in socio-economic changes by utilizing local initiative and in creating new institutions for the same purpose. As the committee was not satisfied with the results of the programme, it recommended the introduction of democratic decentralization in which panchayats were to form the basis of the democracy. The committee also recommended the administrative decentralization under the control of elected bodies for the effective implementation of the developmental programmes.

A three-tier system was to replace the already existing old district boards. The tiers suggested were Gram Panchayat, Panchayat Samiti and Zila Parishad at village level, block level and district level respectively. These tiers have to be linked by indirect elections. The Gram Panchayat at the lowest rung was to be elected by all the adult members of village. All the members of Gram Panchayat were to elect the members of Panchayat Samiti, thus it was to be indirect election, i.e., members of Gram Panchayat shall elect from amongst themselves the members of Panchayat Samiti. The third tier – Zila Parishad – was to replace the district boards. It was to be consisted of the Presidents of Panchayat Samitis, MPs and MLAs along with other officers holding district development departments.

The working of Panchayati Raj during five-year plans, especially first three plans, was satisfactory. A decrease in caste tension was noticeable and the weaker sections were also getting representation in these bodies (Mishra and Singh, 1993: 119). Still various committees were appointed to further improve the functioning of local governments in several areas. On recommendations of various study teams, changes were made from time to time. Besides the creation of Nyaya Panchayats recommendations like strengthening the resources base, encouraging Gram Sabha to play vital role, etc., were made to strengthen the machinery of Panchayati Raj.

But all this had fatal end when centrist tendencies uprooted the whole meaning of decentralized democracy or Panchayati Raj. National emergency took all the powers from local bodies that were important for the development of PRIs. The emergency was lifted in 1977 and Janata Party came to power. After observing the pathetic condition of PRIs, it was decided to appoint a committee under the chairmanship of Ashok Mehta to revive the interest in Panchayati Raj. The committee diagnosed the ills afflicting PRIs and presented its reports in which decentralization of administration was recommended as a necessity. It was called a "new approach to Panchayati Raj" (ibid: 9). The committee observed that weaker sections of the society and most of the institutions are dominated by socially and economically dominant people. Thus, decentralization does not meant only the decentralization of power and people's participation but supporting rural development.

The committee recommended the two-tier system constituting Zila Parishad and Mandal Panchayats consisting the cluster of villages covering almost 15,000 to 20,000 of population. They were to be elected directly. To protect the interests of weaker sections, provision of reservation of seats for Scheduled Castes and Scheduled Tribes in proportion to their population was also made.

Although, states like Andhra Pradesh and Karnataka experimented with this model, but with the change both in central and state level governments, the report could not be implemented fully. However, Panchayati Raj assumed importance and became an important issue of debate since the beginning of 1980s. The Planning Commission appointed a working group in 1983, known as the Hanumantha Rao Committee, which stressed the need for public participation at local level. During the Sixth Plan, it was proposed to give impetus to decentralization. Afterwards, in 1985, the G.V.K. Rao Committee was set up to study the role of Panchayati Raj bodies and their relationships with the proposed administrative set-up (ibid: 129).

Yet another important committee was set up in 1986 under the chairmanship of L.M. Singhvi. The building pressure to review the existing conditions and the reports of various committees, especially of 1980s, led the then Prime Minister Rajiv Gandhi to take initiative in this direction. He called the meetings of various representatives and five workshops were conducted. In these workshops, the suggestion for constitutional provision to make regular elections to PRIs mandatory came up (Narang, 1996: 344).

In 1989, the 64th Amendment Bill was introduced in Lok Sabha in which an attempt was made to assign constitutional status to PRIs. But the Bill was rejected in Rajya Sabha. The reform process then did suffer a setback but by this time the successful working of Panchayati Raj in certain states made political parties to move in favour of decentralization. It was 74th Amendment Bill that was introduced to fulfil this purpose by the National Front government.

The Bill was introduced on the 7th September, 1990 but it could not be taken up for consideration, and got lapsed due to dissolution of Lok Sabha. Thus, both 64th Amendment Bill and 74th Amendment Bill lapsed but they gave impetus to the thinking that PRIs need immediate attention to be reformed and restructured thereby making democracy truly participatory.

The Narsimha Rao government introduced a fresh Bill in Lok Sabha on 16th September, 1991, which was referred to a Joint Select Committee of Parliament in December 1991 for a detailed examination. This committee presented its report in July 1992, and after certain consultations the Bill was passed on 22nd December, 1992. A total of 17 states within a period of four months rectified the Bill and it was sent to the President of India, who accorded his assent on 20th April, 1993. Thus, the 73rd Amendment Act came into effect from 24th April, 1993. Thus, it was only in 1993 that the Panchayati Raj system finally got constitutional status. After part VIII, a separate part IX was added to the Constitution along with Eleventh Schedule enumerating powers and functions of PRIs. The provisions made under the 73rd Amendment Act were the amalgamation of provisions made under 64th and 74th Amendment Bills. It had features like giving importance to Gram Panchayats as well as Gram Sabha, provision of direct elections at all levels of panchayats but elections of chairpersons at the intermediate and district levels shall be indirect. There shall be a uniform pattern of PRIs for all states except where the population is less than 20 lakhs. Reservation policy will be followed and state bodies like State Finance Commission will review the financial status of panchayats and State Election Commission shall be responsible for free and fair elections. Audit shall also be done by state machinery.

The 73rd Constitutional Amendment Act has been made to overcome many of the shortcomings of grassroots level democracy. It was considered the stepping stone in the field of people's participation. In 1996, it was further extended to Scheduled Areas. A Bill was introduced in the parliament and passed, which got assent on December 24, 1996 by the President. The provision of the Panchayats (Extension to the Scheduled Areas) Act, 1996 has extended the Central Act to the Scheduled Areas mentioned under clause (one) of Article 244 of the Constitution. The states of Andhra Pradesh, Himachal Pradesh, Bihar, Maharashtra, Madhya Pradesh, Gujarat, Rajasthan and Orissa are covered under the Fifth Schedule areas. It became mandatory on the part of these states to amend their existing Panchayat Acts in consonance with the Extension Act within a year, i.e., by December 24, 1997 (Mahipal, 2002: 1602).

Thus, to conclude, it can be stated that Indian Constitution did not attempt to make any interpretation of what actually is local self-government. It was only Article 40 of the Constitution that used the term 'self-government' for the village panchayats prior to 73rd amendment. In Articles 243G to 243W, the term 'self-government' has been mentioned but what constitutes self-government has not been stated anywhere. The state legislature is thus the sole determinant of what constitutes 'self-government.' This has been acting as a hurdle in the functioning and strengthening of PRIs. This institution has suffered a lot because of negligence of authorities. However, the 73rd amendment has accorded constitutional status to PRIs making it mandatory for state legislatures to work for reformation of this institution in particular.

Dalit Leadership in the PRIs: A Discussion

The issue of leadership in PRIs has been important since their establishment in 1959. A report of the Ministry of Community Development stated in 1964-65 that "younger and better leadership" was emerging through PR institutions and there was a fairly high degree of satisfaction among people (Mathew, 1994: 6). Another study pointed out that the establishment of Panchayati Raj had given a boost to the emergence of local leadership by creating new seats of power to be filled by the competitive mechanism of democratic elections. This had enabled a large number of people to acquire leadership at the local level, as in the earlier traditional socio-economic set-up they had no access to the political or administrative organs.[5] Similarly, Association of Voluntary Agencies for Rural Development (AVARD) in Rajasthan held that "people felt that they had sufficient power to enable them to mould their future.... They are fully conscious of the fact that such privileges and favours that were formerly under the control of the BDO are now under their control".[6]

However, given the nature of the power structure in the villages, this new crop of leaders emerged mainly from the higher castes and Dalits remained excluded from participation and decision-making. Indeed, this had been anticipated by scholars who had argued that granting of power to local bodies in the prevailing conservative and hierarchical social milieu would lead not only to democracy but also strengthening of the hold of rural upper castes elites upon local affairs. Until recently, few studies devoted much space to the position, role and presence of Dalits in the panchayats leave alone leadership. Most standard histories that adequately trace the development of this institution devote little space to this issue. Much of the literature on PRIs is centred around four broad aspects: (1) decentralization of power and financial responsibilities and its impact, (2) structure of the panchayat institutions, (3) role of the local bureaucracy, and (4) programmes for rural and village development. This was because Dalits were seldom involved in the panchayats in any meaningful fashion, their presence was almost notional and they were not perceived as playing an effective role in the process of social change and development at the local level. In some states, to overcome the problem of under-representation of Dalits in the panchayats, co-option in place of election was tried out as an alternative arrangement in the 1970s. Some prominent members of local panchayats from the lower castes were co-opted but experience revealed that this did not fill the gap (Kumar, 1999). The Ashok Mehta Committee report held that "the system of co-option through nomination of SCs/STs has been so manipulated that the nominated/co-opted members are generally allied in the dominant faction" (Ashok Mehta Committee, 1978: 9).

The official position on the participation of weaker sections was an 'incremental' one that gradual change due to decentralization of powers and responsibilities would lead to their active participation. It was hoped that implementation of land reforms, establishment of community development and Panchayati Raj and rapid agricultural development would over time democratize the village structure and the panchayats. In fact, the Balwantrai Mehta Committee's report, which led to the establishment of Panchayati Raj in 1959, was keen to avoid immediate competition at the grassroots. It recommended that "efforts should be made to ensure that elections to the village panchayats are made as far as possible by the general consent of the people and the bitterness and hostility created by elections is avoided. The membership of the village panchayats should be regarded as an opportunity for service to the people which should be undertaken by the best men in the village rather than as a means for obtaining power and prestige" (Mehta, 1957: 2.36). However, as a recent study points out, these hopes were belied as the panchayats were captured by autocratic and invariably corrupt leaders in the village (Lieten and Srivastava, 1999: 22).

A few studies in the 1960s and 1970s also did divert attention towards the position of Dalits in the panchayats. For example, Murthy (1969) found that if the Sarpanch, who holds a key position in implementing programmes for Dalits and STs, was directly elected by the people and not indirectly by the members of the panchayat, then, the interests of these groups could be better secured. Similarly, writing in the early 1970s, Parvathamma (1975) pointed out that political representation at the local level had not helped to improve the socio-economic position of Dalits due to built-in drawbacks which prevented them from being vocal and asserting themselves such as poverty, illiteracy, ignorance and dependence upon the upper castes and above all their low position in the caste hierarchy. Others also argued that PRIs had not been able to devote any special attention to Dalits because of limited financial resources due to which these institutions did not exhibit any special solicitude for the welfare of the weaker sections (Ali, 1964). Adiseshiah (1964) observed that well-to-do Pradhans from the higher castes were able to manipulate resources given to panchayats for welfare of the Dalits and direct them towards other less deserving persons. Consequently, the most deserving cases did not receive the benefits meant for them. Even after seats were reserved for Dalits in some states in the mid-1980s, many studies held that Dalits continued to be passive participants in panchayats because they lacked the essential prerequisites of education and sufficient income (Gurumurthy, 1987). However, by the mid-1980s, in UP, a study documented important changes taking place in UP society – the rise of a new educated, better off and development-oriented set of leaders from among the Dalits belonging to largely landless families. Due to exposure to mass media, political awareness and political participation were increasing though their abilities were not well developed. Their entry into the panchayats was possible in many cases due to strong support from their caste members and village factions. Standing halfway between tradition and modernity, they were development oriented but were not able to introduce much change due to the oppressive practices of the higher castes and classes (Singh, 1985).

The Ashok Mehta Committee, set up to suggest ways to reinvigorate panchayats in the late 1970s, agreed that the local institutions had been dominated by the economically and socially privileged sections of society and as such had provided little benefits to the poorer and disadvantaged sections. But, in marked similarity to official thinking, it argued that the democratization process as a component of modernization would "destabilize traditional leadership in the long run" (Mehta, 1978:1). It held that despite the failures of PR, this process had begun and generated a new leadership that was both younger as well as "modernistic and pro-social change in outlook" (ibid). However, the Ashok Mehta Committee recognized that democratization of the panchayat required "active participation of women" and "special reservation of seats for the weaker sections, namely, the SCs and STs". Although, the report could not be implemented by the central government due to the collapse of the Janata government, some state governments, e.g., West Bengal, Karnataka and Andhra Pradesh adopted its recommendations including that of reservations for the weaker sections. It was the success of these state governments in providing representation and inclusion, if not participation in decision-making, to the weaker sections that eventually led to the 64th and finally the 73rd constitutional amendment, which gave special representation to women, Dalits and STs. In fact, in many respects the 73rd constitutional amendment was an implementation of the 1977 proposals (Lieten and Srivastava, 1999: 25).

The Karnataka experiment, initiated by the Janata Party when it came to power in January 1987, based on the recommendations of the Ashoka Mehta Committee, lasted till the end of 1991 when the Congress government was elected which abandoned it (Crook and Manor, 1998: 23). Here, 25 per cent of the seats in all councils were reserved for women and a minimum of 18 per cent for members of the Dalits and tribes. Provision was also made for the 'backward classes' when no members of these groups were elected to the council, two such persons were to be appointed by the government. The study showed that democratic decentralization achieved considerable success but the extent to which the Dalits gained from it remain doubtful. The Gram Sabha did not serve as an effective formal device to promote grassroots participation and the tiny proportion of Dalits that attended did not inspire confidence in its functioning (ibid: 31). But, the study suggested that in states where the Dalits have asserted themselves, the chances of reservation of seats for this group could be useful. Dalits voted in only slightly smaller numbers, were active in campaigning, they believed the elections were fair and had fairly high level of participation in village associations. Elected Dalit members approached members of the mandal and district councils with petitions. However, the study shows that Dalit councillors did not achieve much through participation - individually or collectively. In some district councils, where a particular Dalit member was active, or the higher castes were sympathetic, they could through active participation wrest benefits for their community. But, at the mandal level, which had largely uneducated members and stood close to the village level, the study points out that "it was virtually impossible for Dalit representatives to influence events"(ibid). In a constituency that had only about 400 electors low-caste voters could not remain anonymous about who they had voted for and fear of retribution remained. Second, since the mandal councils played a seminal role in distributing resources, implementing many programmes and selecting beneficiaries, the better off sections often prevented the poorer and disadvantaged groups from gaining anything (ibid: 39). In fact, the whole cultural milieu in the local arenas was weighed against assertiveness from low-status groups: while the higher castes routinely prevented the Dalits from benefiting, the latter remained utterly passive. The level of responsiveness towards Dalit elected members from the district level bureaucrats and politicians was mixed. In some places, they did gain due to sympathetic leaders from the 'higher castes' but on the whole they gained very little. In fact, the study points out that the net effect was to enhance the share of resources going to the prosperous groups at the expense of the poor, which placed the Dalits in a less advantageous position than before (ibid: 77).

By the late 1980s, there was consensus that the panchayats were captured by the upper castes/classes in the countryside and the weaker sections remained marginalised. The existing literature shows that panchayat institutions at the village, block and district level were captured by the upper castes/classes (Jha and Mathur, 1999). Elections were not held regularly and when held the upper castes/classes in the village managed to capture power, leaving little room for representation for the 'lower castes' that were excluded from participation. Elections were rather the means by which the former were able to consolidate their power in the countryside (Khanna, 1994). Decisions were made by the higher castes and better off sections and the disadvantaged groups were marginalized.

Following the 73rd amendment, there has been greater interest in the emerging Dalit leadership in panchayats due to reservation of seats. A number of studies point to a younger and better educated leadership, many of whom own land though some are landless labourers also. Many of them by the end of 1990s have gained political experience having been elected for the second or third time and have shown interest in agricultural development (Shymala, 2001). Other studies that concentrated on the awareness of the new leaders about panchayat programmes found that their knowledge about the existing governmental schemes, sources of finances, standing committees was reasonably high, but their ability to take decisions and manage responsibility was not high. However, they argued that the process of incorporation of Dalits at the grassroots had begun. The reservation policy had altered the rural power structure in favour of the marginalized but the ability of the first generation leaders needed to be fully developed, which, it was felt, required training – a point which many studies have underlined (Sheshadri and Azim, 2001; Aziz, 1994). Others have pointed out that wherever the pace of economic change and political mobilization is fast Dalits have questioned the existing patterns of power creating conflict (Pai, 2004), whereas economic dependence allows the continuance of older structures of dominance and power within the panchayats (Lele, 2001). Pundir (1995), in a study of four areas located in eastern and western UP, found that numerical superiority of the Dalit population is an important factor leading to higher levels of participation.

These studies show that reservation has enabled Dalits to enter into the panchayats and thus reservation has proved to be a major social intervention to empower the panchayat representatives belonging to the disadvantaged sections without which they would not have been able to enter into the PRIs. However, their level of participation in decision-making, as well as formulation and implementation of schemes, is not very encouraging. A study in Orissa found that elected representatives were not able to properly articulate group-specific interests or to exercise their own judgement in panchayat, decision-making, thus bringing into question the very notion of representation of marginalized groups through affirmative action (Patnaik, 2005) Examining the power structure, class relations and pattern of leadership, a study of a village in West Bengal found that bureaucratic patronage and caste-based hierarchy continue to frustrate attempts on the part of leaders to introduce change. They concluded that there had been little 'structural change' in terms of leadership (Chakraborty and Bhattacharyya, 1993).

The 73rd Constitutional Amendment while granting reservations to Dalits, has made it compulsory that one-third of the seats reserved for them be filled by Dalit women. The conformity legislations in the states have also reiterated this provision. While there is a burgeoning literature on the role played by women representatives in the new panchayats[7] little attention has been paid to Dalit women elected on reserved seats, specially those elected as Sarpanchas. Special problems faced by these women have not been the subject of much scholarly or official scrutiny. Existing studies suggest that the impact of reservations has been differential. In states where the social status of women has traditionally been better and levels of literacy, status in society and participation in the workforce are higher, women have been able to take advantage of this measure. In Andhra Pradesh, Karnataka and Maharashtra, even prior to the new legislation, women had contested elections, occupied reserved positions and contributed to the functioning of panchayats. In all women panchayats, this was even more clearly recognizable. Quite a few studies had pointed out the difference that women members made to the nature of the decisions and the process by which they were formulated. Power meant giving priority to issues like drinking water supply, installation of hand pumps, construction of toilets, village wells and roads, appointment of teachers, closing of liquor shops etc. There were instances, as in Vitner village in Jalgaon district (Maharashtra), where women got playgrounds built, land transferred to 127 women from their husband's share and toilets constructed in the Dalit areas. Women in Pidghara (MP) went for a 27-point action plan that took up the building of educational and other community-based infrastructure. The experience and action agenda of the seven-member panchayat of Brahmanghar of Pune was also similar (Kaushik, 1995: 5). In such states, the granting of reservations has helped strengthen the position of Dalit women.

In other parts of the country, where women's position in the family and society and participation in public affairs has traditionally been low as in the states in the northern plains, the reservation measure has not caused much change. The impact of this measure has been much slower. A study argues that reservation alone cannot change the status of women and enable their participation in local bodies. The position of women and the perception that they have little knowledge about, and are incapable of taking part in public affairs, even of independent voting, remains strong. The pradhanis in the study were mere namesake representatives of the male members of the household (Pai, 2000: 127).

In some states, there has been little or no acceptance of reservation for the lower castes by the upper castes in the village. This has resulted in atrocities against panchayat members including women. Four case studies from Madhya Pradesh reveal that the power structure in villages in this state remains oppressive. Dalit women and men who stood for election were beaten, raped and ill-treated and their land grabbed by members of the higher castes who were not prepared to relinquish power to the lower castes. An easier method to retain power is to put up proxy candidates but keep the control in the hands of the dominant castes, always men. The incapacity of women, particularly Dalit women, to assert their rights is at the root of the problem. The study showed that reservation for Dalits, particularly for women, is accepted in form but seldom in substance. Any change in the status quo is resisted, sometimes violently (Mathew and Nayak, 1996: 1771). This points to the limitations as well as the possibilities of state intervention without the necessary concurrent social support systems. Similar experiences have been reported from Tamil Nadu, Rajasthan and Bihar (Mathew, 2004:256; Nayak, 1996).

Dalit women have also faced many problems in performing their duties due to illiteracy, lack of information and dependency on the male members of their families. An important obstacle is no-confidence motions against Dalit women pradhans by the dominant sections who are unable to accept that power has been given into the hands of the poorer and disadvantaged women (Mahipal, 1998).

However, few systematic studies of Dalit Sarpanchas and Panchas have been carried out which enable us to draw conclusions about the nature of the emerging leadership and the extent of their participation. It is this gap that present study hopes to fill.

Framework of the Study

The framework used in this study for analysis of Dalit leadership includes three concepts: representation, inclusion and participation. Through the device of reservation, Dalits have been provided for the first time an opportunity for effective representation in panchayats. In recent years, with interest in the representation of minorities and disadvantaged groups worldwide, existing literature argues that disadvantaged groups prefer to be represented by individuals who in their own backgrounds 'mirror' the typical experiences and outward manifestations of belonging to the disadvantaged group (Mansbridge, 2000: 99). In a representative democracy, representatives are expected to serve as instruments of communication and consultation with their constituents as well as other interest groups. They are also expected to put forward issues of salience to their constituents, which have not yet been debated. But members of disadvantaged groups embedded in a tradition of domination and subordination are often unable to be part of this deliberative process due to the existence of prejudice on the part of the dominant group and distrust on the part of the subordinate group. Members of subordinate groups may thus find that "effective substantive representation" depends on their being represented by member of their own group, with whom they can communicate easily and by whom they can reasonably expect to be better understood (ibid). Thus, an important research question in our empirical studies is how far reservation has provided effective representation to social groups so far denied the same.

The second related question is how far the granting of reservations, which has changed the social composition of panchayats, has promoted the inclusion of the disadvantaged sections excluded so far. Representatives who belong to the disadvantaged group can change the "social meaning of membership" through their very presence and actions in the decision-making institution through what has been described as the "politics of presence". This has the advantage that it increases the *de facto* legitimacy of the political system for the members of this group as it removes their earlier exclusion or marginalization. This positive effect on political status is particularly important when the polity has a history of exclusion of the group from the mainstream social and political life. Such exclusion usually leaves historical traces of the dominant culture's past conclusion that members of the group so specified were not fit to rule.

The third question is have the new panchayats given a blow to the traditional unequal rural power structures based on land and ritual status, and provided greater room for participation and involvement in decision-making by the deprived sections. In brief, the study examines through this threefold framework, whether there has been democratisation of the panchayats.

In our study, leadership is viewed as a process in which the followers and the leaders of the group interact with each other in a given context. It is a group process through which individuals initiate activities for achieving the common objectives of the group or community by working together, stimulating each other, supplementing abilities and resources, and evolving an effective organizational and hierarchical plan. The relationship between the leaders and the followers is one of the several forms of interpersonal relationships formed to satisfy some of the defined needs of the leaders and the followers. The behaviour of one is generally influenced by the behaviour of the other and the behaviour of both is determined by the nature and structure of the social structure in which they interact. As Wood points out, "almost certainly for rural India and probably for India as a whole, it will be necessary for social scientists to explore leadership structure by looking for processes rather than for persons" (1960: 381). While this process is important in all institutions, as our study will show, it holds special importance for Dalits in the new panchayats.

This empirical study covers four states in North India. In Haryana and Uttar Pradesh (UP) one district and in Himachal Pradesh and Madhya Pradesh (MP) two districts were selected for study. In all the selected states, the percentage of Dalits in the population is higher than the all-India average except in MP. However, the two districts selected for study in MP are in the northern region where Dalits are concentrated in large numbers. There are marked differences in the socio-economic and political contexts in which panchayats function in the four selected states. This allows us to understand the role played by Dalit leaders in panchayats embedded in differing contexts. A second factor is that political consciousness among Dalits has been increasing since the colonial period and in the post-independence period but the pace of change has been different in different regions of India leading to uneven development across the subcontinent in the post-independence period. The process of change has been faster in some regions and slower in others creating significant differences which have impacted on the functioning of panchayats.

Haryana is an agriculturally prosperous state where Dalits are better off than in UP and MP as poverty levels are lower and employment is higher due to agricultural prosperity. A recent report, which provides a profile of the states, shows that the percentage of rural population below the poverty line in 1993-94 was 28 per cent, while in UP and MP it was 42 per cent and 41 per cent respectively (Shariff, 1999: 41). Among 16 states, Haryana with a per capita income of Rs 6,368 ranked second, while UP was ranked eleventh with Rs 4,185, Himachal

Pradesh twelfth with Rs 4,168 and MP thirteenth with Rs 4,166 (ibid: 25). In the rural areas in all states, Dalits form a substantial part of the agricultural labour force. Agricultural wages are higher in Haryana, the average annual wage income being Rs 7,012, while in the remaining three states it is between Rs 2 to 4 thousand only. However, in Haryana, the literacy rate among Dalits is only 39.22 per cent and drops to 24.15 among Dalit women. Haryana also ranks low in human development: the sex ratio being only 861 per thousand compared to 970 in Himachal Pradesh. Moreover, it is a state that is backward in terms of attitudes towards Dalits. A large number of atrocities have been perpetuated on Dalits by the middle castes such as Jats and Gujars and the state also suffers from a democratic deficit.

Both MP and UP are economically backward states where the Dalits are very poor. Literacy levels are low, landlessness is high and a large number of Dalits are below the poverty line. Both untouchability and discrimination are present and hamper the functioning of the panchayats. The village power structure is still skewed in favour of the traditionally landowning castes/classes, mainly the OBCs. Caste atrocities, particularly in UP, are as high as in Haryana. However, UP has experienced since the mid-1980s a strong wave of Dalit assertion under the leadership of the Bahujan Samaj Party (BSP). The party aims at providing self-respect and dignity to Dalits. Under its protection, Dalits have been able to vote and the party has captured power in the state. However, whether this has helped Dalits in the panchayats needs to be investigated as they remain at the mercy of the upper castes in the villages. In MP, in the northern districts including Satna selected for this study, the BSP has been able to make inroads from neighbouring UP and in the 1990s has been able to gain seats. This has raised the level of political awareness and the Congress government under Digvijay Singh took a number of measures to help the Dalits.

In contrast, in Himachal Pradesh, the caste system has traditionally not been as oppressive as in the north Indian plains although untouchability has been practised. Today, social distance is maintained but only in very few areas of private life and social discrimination does not affect the functioning of the panchayats. Here, landholding pattern is also less skewed and horticulture is a common occupation practised by all caste groups. More rapid economic development in recent years as well as a sharp rise in literacy, better educational attainments and employment among Dalits have given more confidence than in many other states. The position of women, including Dalit women, is better than in the plains areas. Literacy rates are much higher in Himachal Pradesh than in the other states selected for the present study, being 53.20 per cent among men and 41.02 per cent among women. Consequently, although much more change is needed, among the selected states, the positive impact of reservations on the role of Dalits in panchayats is seen in this state. Thus, the selected panchayats are located in differing socio-economic and political contexts. This study investigates - given the conditions in each of these states - how far Dalits have been able to participate meaningfully in the new panchayats.

Using the empirical materials from the fieldwork, the study first provides a profile of the emerging Dalit leadership in the panchayats in the different states and then examines the extent to which Dalits, including Dalit women, have been included in the decision-making system of the panchayats. Some of the issues based on the empirical data examined are: in the existing power structure, do the elected Dalit Sarpanchas play a significant role, or do they act as dictated by the higher castes?, what are the types of problems faced by Dalit Sarpanchas in the execution of their duty?, does illiteracy or low educational background constitute a problem?, do they receive any training?, has there been real devolution of power and finances downward so that Dalit Sarpanchas can make an impact?, are women proxies for their husbands or have they begun to play a role in the panchayats?, and do women and Dalits merely attend or do they participate in decision-making thereby making a difference to the conditions of Dalits in the villages.

The study identifies some 'enabling factors' that help in the emergence of Dalit leadership. Three factors are responsible for the emergence of a new crop of Dalit leaders in the new panchayats. They are: rise in literacy and educational attainments, improvement in economic condition and political mobilization. In regions where Dalits have been able to gain some education and their economic condition has improved, they have overcome to some extent exclusion and upper/middle caste domination in the panchayats. But, where they are poor and dependent upon caste-Hindus for their livelihood, they are unable to develop 'independent thinking', their acts are motivated by dominant castes and so have not been able to provide leadership (Kumar, 1999). Political mobilization by either a political party or a younger and assertive leadership has been an important factor even in regions where Dalits are poor as it provides them self-confidence and strength to demand a share in political decision-making and the fruits of economic development at the local level.

Besides this introductory chapter, the study is divided into five chapters. Four chapters are devoted to the examination of the working of the PRIs based upon the field study in sample districts and villages in the four selected states. They also examine the extent to which Dalits have been able to gain representation and participation in the new panchayats and focus upon the problems encountered by them. Chapter five attempts a brief comparative analysis of the role played by the emerging Dalit leadership in the selected states and attempts to identify the factors that have helped/hindered in the inclusion and effective participation of Dalits in the new panchayats. This allows the study in the concluding chapter to put forward some policy recommendations, which could lead to further democratization of panchayats.

Notes

1. The term 'Dalit' has been used throughout the study interchangeably with the legal term 'Scheduled Caste'.
2. The figures are from the CSDS survey, see the explanation provided in Pushpendra (1999), for the high figures as against the figures given by the Election Commission.
3. For details see the special issue on 'Scheduled Castes' of *The Journal of Political Economy*, 2000.
4. On this issue, see Gulati (2000).
5. L.P. Shukla in Mathew (1994).
6. Association of Voluntary Agencies for Rural Development quoted in Mathew (1994: 7).
7. For details see, Buch, Jain and Chaudhary, 1999, *Women in Panchayati Raj in Madhya Pradesh* (Mimeo), Mahila Chetna Manch, Bhopal.

2

Dalit Leadership in Panchayats in Himachal Pradesh

A Case Study of Shimla and Sirmaur

Himachal Pradesh has a distinct socio-cultural and economic identity different from the northern states lying in the plains area. In contrast to our selected states of UP and MP it is more prosperous and highly literate. It is ahead of Haryana in terms of not only literacy but also human development and particularly the status of women. Thus, it enables us to test whether social and economic development undermines caste-based inequalities and has facilitated the emergence of leadership among the Dalits elected to the new panchayats.

Himachal Pradesh (HP) is a small state, a hilly region having an area of about 55,673 square kilometres. The entire state is divided into three ranges, namely, Lower, Middle and Upper Himalayas. According to 2001 census, it has a population of about 60,77,248 with a density of 109 persons per square kilometre with about 90.21 per cent of the population of the state residing in the rural areas. It is presently divided into 12 districts, 75 tehsils, 75 developmental blocks and 20,118 villages. Scheduled Castes (SCs) constitute 25.34 per cent of the total population while about 4.22 per cent are Schedule Tribes

(STs). The percentage of SCs to the total population is highest in the middle hills, i.e., Solan, Sirmaur, Mandi and Shimla which is where our sample regions fall. Solan has the highest followed closely by Sirmaur. In the upper and lower hills the percentage of SCs is low.

HP is a prosperous state and the economic condition of people is much better than in UP and MP. Per capita income at current prices estimated in 1995-96 is Rs 8,747. It is a prosperous state with about 28 per cent of the population below the poverty line. It is an agro-based state where about 71 per cent of employed workers are engaged in agricultural pursuits. The total cultivated area is about 61 per cent out of which only 81 per cent is the net area sown. Horticulture is a major source of income for upper hill areas. Every year, about 6,000 to 7,000 hectares of land are brought under horticulture. Traditionally, horticulture was a symbol of higher status but today, as our study will show, not only Rajputs and Brahmins but Dalits also have taken to horticulture making it a common vocation without any caste barriers and which has provided mobility to the lower castes. Although, the upper castes own more land, their holdings are small and there are no big landlords in the region. The state has played an important role in promoting horticulture and 113 state nurseries and 800 private plantation nurseries have been registered, cold storages have been established and the state government is providing subsidies to farmers, of which up to 50 per cent is being provided to farmers belonging to SCs and STs, up to 25 per cent to small farmers and up to 33.3 per cent to middle class farmers. The other significant areas contributing to Himachal's economy are forestry and hydropower with the production of 2,995 MW till 1997. Industrialization has also started taking its root in the last decades with 167 medium and large-scale industries. Tourism has also been given priority as an industry.

The population of Himachal Pradesh is mainly Hindu consisting of upper caste Brahmins and Rajputs. Dalits, who constitute 24 per cent of the population, are divided into two sub-castes: Kalis in upper areas and Chamars in the lower. The Scheduled Tribes mainly reside in Kinnaur, Lauhaul-Spiti and Chamba and are divided into Negis, Lahaulas, and Gaddies. Caste and untouchability play a very important role in the functioning of panchayats in India. In HP, there is less discrimination than in the three other states selected for study. Whatever discrimination is there, it is found in the upper areas of the state where the practice of untouchability is found even today rather than in the lower areas. The reasons perhaps lie in the fact that economic differences between Dalits and non-Dalits are more in the former where Dalits are poor whereas the differences in the latter region are much less.

Himachal Pradesh has a literacy rate of about 73.13 per cent, which is above the national average and much higher than in other northern states. Although, disparity in male-female literacy ratio persists, it is the second state of India to achieve a high level of literacy after Kerala. Males and females both are educated as males have literacy rate of about 86.02 per cent and females 68.08 per cent. Even in rural areas the literacy rate of females is 66.30 per cent and of males is 85.20 per cent. Despite being predominantly rural, the outlook of the people is modern due to the high literacy rates and comparative male-female literacy rates. As we shall see this impacts upon the social structure and the role played by Dalits in the panchayats. HP also has a good record of provision of social welfare particularly for the weaker sections of society. The state has adequate health centres, safe drinking water to all and almost every village is electrified and has telephone facilities as well.

PRIs and the Sample Districts

Formed on April 15, 1948 with the merger of about 30 princely states of Shimla and others in the Himalayan region, Himachal Pradesh was not immediately accorded full statehood, hence, the legislature was also not present at that time. After the integration, a major problem was the organization of these princely states into tehsils and districts. The bigger states like

Chamba and Sirmaur were converted into districts with the same name, whereas, the states of Mandi and Suket were integrated to form Mandi district. Twenty-six Shimla hill states, including their tributaries, were integrated to form Mahasu district, probably named after the name of Mahasu – a deity widely worshipped in the area. In 1966, the Punjab hill areas were integrated with Himachal Pradesh, which was granted statehood on January 25, 1971.

In 1948, Himachal Pradesh adopted the Punjab Village Panchayat Act, 1939. It had only four districts and in 1949, 132 panchayats were established. However, panchayats have a long history in the region as they were established as early as 1908, in the Bilaspur region of the present state by Raja Bijai Chand. Today, the lower Himalayas comprising districts of Bilaspur, Hamirpur, Kangra and Una have a total of 1,264 panchayats and 7,974 wards.

The record of the state government in the setting up and working of panchayats has been better than in many other states. When the Balwantrai Mehta Committee report was implemented in the country, panchayats at the tehsil level were already functioning in HP. Under the HP Panchayati Raj Act, 1968, a two-tier panchayat system was introduced throughout the state. More important in this system was if no SCs were elected to the panchayats, they could be co-opted. In 1994 itself, with a view to bringing the law relating to panchayats in conformity with the provision of the 73rd constitutional amendment, the HP Panchayati Raj Act, 1994 was enacted. Under this Act, the Middle Himalayas, consisting of districts Mandi, Shimla, Sirmaur and Solan, have 1,110 panchayats and 7,103 wards. The Upper Himalayan region has 548 panchayats and 3,187 wards (Mohapatra, 2002). The growth of the PRIs in the state has been considerable during the last three decades. The number increased from 2,035 in 1972 to 3,037 in 2000. Due to the high percentage of SCs in the population, the share of reserved seats is, as Table 1.1 shows, quite substantial. It is 20.53 per cent in Gram Panchayats, 16.85 per cent in

Panchayat Samitis and 18.25 per cent in Zila Parishads. For SC women the share of reserved seats is 8.27, 8.66 and 7.93 per cent respectively. In brief, more than 50 per cent of the total seats are reserved for SC, ST and women candidates in the PRIs in HP. This pattern of reserved seats exceeding open seats is clearly seen at the district level in Table 1.2 that provides the district-wise seat reservation for SCs, STs and women. Thus, there has been considerable devolution of power through reservation to the weaker sections in HP under the complimentary legislation. More important for our purposes, care has been taken to extend reservation to leadership positions in the new panchayats. As per the central and state legislation, the State Election Commission was constituted in April 1994. All panchayat bodies constituted under the earlier system were dissolved and two elections have been held to panchayat bodies in HP – the first in December 1995 and the second in December 2000.

In Himachal Pradesh, two districts selected for the field study were Shimla and Sirmaur. Two considerations guided the choice of districts. First, both have a high concentration of SCs in the population: Shimla has 26 per cent while Sirmaur has 30.17 per cent. Although, Solan district has 31.27 per cent SC population but in social and economic terms, the district is more developed than Sirmaur, which led to the choice of the latter. Second, Shimla is a well-developed and important district, while Sirmaur is socio-economically backward. This allowed us to examine whether economic development together with literacy has led to the rise of an effective Dalit leadership in regions like Shimla.

Sample Districts

Shimla, the capital of Himachal Pradesh, has been associated with many important events of Indian history. It was the summer capital of the British government in India and witnessed many important events and conferences at which important decisions were made. Shimla also played an important part in the struggle for independence. The Indian National Congress and Praja Mandalists started their activities from Shimla. In 1945-46 Jawahar Lal Nehru, Maulana Abdul Kalam Azad, Sardar Vallabh Bhai Patel, M.A. Jinnah and other prominent leaders visited Shimla to attend the Shimla Conference. The Independence Act, 1947 was signed in Shimla by the then Governor General Mountbatten. The famous 1972 Shimla Agreement between India and Pakistan was also signed in Shimla. Thus, the panchayats in this district have greater political consciousness than those in the interior.

Occupying the eastern part of the state, Shimla is a relatively large district, covering 9.22 per cent of the total area with state headquarters at Shimla. Areas-wise, the district ranks sixth among all the districts in the state. It is a highly urban district, which includes, besides Shimla town, other towns such as Theog, Kasumpti, Kotkhai, Jubble, Rohroo, Narkanda, Kumarsain and Rampur. Sutlej, Pabar and Giri are the major rivers of this district and Dodarakawar valley of tons catchment also forms a part of this district. As per 2001 census, the population of Shimla district is 7,21,745, which is 11.87 per cent of the total population (60,77,248) of the state. Out of which 3,80,244 are males and 3,41,501 are females. As much as 5,54,912 persons live in the rural area while 1,66,833 in the urban area. Shimla district comprises 2,597 villages, of which 2,311 are inhabited and 286 are uninhabited. The percentage of SCs in the district is 27.13 per cent and of STs, it is 0.71 per cent. The Hindus constitute a pre-dominant majority while the other religious groups are Muslims, Christians, Sikhs, Buddhists and Jains. The main castes in the district are Brahmins, Rajputs, Dalits and other backward castes (OBCs).

The economy of the district is based on agriculture, horticulture, forests, hydel power and tourism. Horticulture in the district is playing a vital role in improving the socio-economic conditions of the rural people. Lying in the apple belt of the state, it is the most dominant fruit crop in the district. The area under the apple crop is steadily increasing. About 60 per cent of the apples of Himachal Pradesh come from district Shimla. Tourism also provides a boost to the local economy of the district.

Shimla was originally part of Mahasu district formed in 1948 by integrating 26 Shimla hill states into 11 tehsils. In 1966, when the Punjab hill areas were integrated with Himachal Pradesh, four new districts, viz., Kangra, Kulu, Lahaul and Spiti, apart from Shimla, were formed. Shimla district had comprised tehsils, namely, Shimla, Kandaghat and Nalagarh. After attaining the statehood on January 25, 1971, Mahasu and Shimla districts were reorganized into Shimla and Solan districts. Shimla district, with its headquarters at Shimla, comprised the area of Shimla tehsil (Kasumpti tehsil was merged with Shimla tehsil), Theog, Rampur, Chopal, Jubbal and Rohroo tehsils and Kumarsain, Suni and Kotkhai sub-tehsils. The present Shimla district is divided into seven sub-divisions, 11 tehsils, and 39 development blocks.

A total of four blocks were selected for the present study one in Shimla and three in Sirmaur district. Rohroo block in Shimla district is a large block and lies close to a big urban conglomeration and is better developed in contrast to Rajgarh, Nahan and Paonta blocks in Sirmaur, which lie more in the interior and are comparatively not as well developed and connected. The two locales provide two contrasting contexts for studying the emerging Dalit leadership in the new panchayats.

Rohroo Block: A Profile

Rohroo block in district Shimla is located at a distance of 110 km from Shimla town. It has 29 gram panchayats and 181 ward panchayats. The total area of Rohroo block, which has 153 villages, is 30,342 hectares. As per the records available in the office of BDO, Rohroo as on 31st December, 2002, it has a population of 55,512 persons with males comprising 28,214 and females 27,298. The population of OBC is 473, of which 224 are males and 249 females. The male population (50.82%) of the

Table 1.1

Sex and category-wise population of panchayats in Rohroo block (District Shimla, HP)

S. No.	Name of Gram Panchayat	General			SC			OBC			Grand Total		
		Male	Female	Total	Male	Female	Total	Male	Female	Total	Male	Female	Total
1.	Arhal	1040	1057	2097	599	625	1224	26	24	50	1665	1706	3371
2.	Banchhunch	1041	965	2006	423	403	826	-	-	-	1464	1368	2832
3.	Bhaloon	654	620	1274	126	129	255	-	-	-	780	749	1529
4.	BhamnoIi	487	452	939	156	141	297	-	-	-	643	593	1236
5.	Bashla	347	309	656	167	145	312	-	-	-	514	454	968
6.	BrasIi	774	772	1546	247	251	498	-	-	-	1021	1023	2044
7.	Dalgaon	498	481	979	301	308	609	-	-	-	799	789	1588
8.	Dharara	878	838	1716	357	370	727	-	-	-	1235	1208	2443
9.	Hanstari	301	306	607	140	152	292	-	-	-	441	458	899
10.	Jagothi	665	639	1304	238	228	466	-	-	-	903	867	1770
11.	Kadivan	280	255	535	114	102	216	-	-	-	394	357	751
12.	Karalash	421	389	819	446	565	1011	-	-	-	867	954	1821
13.	Karasa	1023	945	1968	392	376	768	-	-	-	1415	1321	2736
14.	Karchhari	487	465	952	353	381	734	-	-	-	840	846	1686

Contd...

Contd...

15.	Katlah	725	707	1432	226	229	455	-	-	-	951	936	1887
16.	Khangteri	630	601	1231	462	418	880	-	-	-	1092	1019	2111
17.	Kutara	565	540	1105	559	537	1096	-	-	-	1124	1077	2201
18.	Kuthari	398	339	737	283	306	589	-	-	-	681	645	1326
19.	Lower Koti	948	885	1833	459	453	912	-	-	-	1407	1338	2745
20.	Munchhara	421	409	830	209	221	430	-	-	-	630	630	1260
21.	Puiarali-3	475	491	967	293	317	610	-	-	-	768	809	1377
22.	Puiarali-4	547	508	1055	383	366	749	-	-	-	930	874	1804
23.	Summer Kot	769	722	1491	325	300	625	-	-	-	1094	1022	2116
24.	SamoIi	578	519	1097	272	253	525	-	-	-	850	772	1622
25.	Shekhal	374	356	730	341	301	642	71	79	150	786	736	1522
26.	Sharontha	318	289	607	226	209	435	-	-	-	544	498	1042
27.	Sheel	1127	1085	2212	481	466	947	-	-	-	1608	1551	3159
28.	Rantari (Seema)	590	550	1140	363	356	719	127	146	273	'1080	1052	2132
29.	Tikkar	1110	1074	2184	578	572	1150	-	-	-	1688	1646	3334
	Grand Total	18471	17569	36034	9519	9480	18999	224	249	473	28214	27298	55512

Source: Secretary, Block Development Office, Rohroo.

tehsil is slightly higher than the female population except in three panchayats, namely, Arhal, Hanstari and Pujarli (Table 1.1). The population of SCs is 34.22 per cent of the total population comprising 17.14 per cent males and 17.07 per cent females. The OBCs are less than one per cent of the population and are concentrated in four panchayats of the sample area. It is the only category in which aggregate population of females exceeds to males in the entire block.

Surrounded by Rampur in the north, Jubbal in the south, Chohara in the east and Kotkhai in the west, the Rahroo block touches the boundary of all the above tehsils and blocks of Shimla district. Rohroo town is the central place for all the social, political and economic activities of the people of the area. All the panchayats of this block are connected by road with Rohroo town. The people from villages frequently visit Rohroo to meet their daily requirements and also sometimes in connection with some work in government offices. Rohroo town, apart from being a block headquarters, is also a sub-divisional headquarters of Rohroo, Jubbal and Chohara blocks. All the important government offices such as the Sub-Judge office, BDO office, PWD circle, government hospital, police station, government degree college, government polytechnic college, transport and communication offices, revenue office, etc., are situated at Rohroo. Apart from Rohroo, Tikkar, Pujarli Arhal, Samarkot and Khadrala are the other semi-urban townships of the area.

Out of the 29 panchayats in Rohroo, seven are reserved for women, six for SC males, three for SC females and the remaining 13 for the general category. Out of these, a sample of 12 panchayats was selected for field study. A profile of the population in these panchayats in terms of SCs, STs and women is provided in Table 1.1a. Overall, the general population in the sampled panchayats is 66.16 per cent of the total population with SC constituting 32.05 per cent. The overall male population in these panchayats is 50.75 per cent. In Karchari panchayat, the percentage of SCs is the highest.

Table 1.1a

Sex and category-wise percentage of population in Panchayats in Rohroo block (District Shimla, HP)

S. No.	Name of Gram Panchayat	General			SC			OBC			Grand Total		
		Male	*Female*	*Total*	*Male*	*Female*	*Total*	*Male*	*Female*	*Total*	*Male*	*Female*	*Total*
1.	Arhal	30.851	31.356	62.207	17.769	18.540	36.310	0.771	0.712	1.483	49.392	50.608	100.00
2.	Banchhunch	36.758	34.075	70.833	14.936	14.230	29.167	0.000	0.000	0.000	51.695	48.305	100.00
3.	Bhaloon	42.773	40.549	83.322	8.241	8.437	16.678	0.000	0.000	0.000	51.014	48.986	100.00
4.	Bhamnoli	39.401	36.570	75.971	12.621	11.408	24.029	0.000	0.000	0.000	52.023	47.977	100.00
5.	Bashla	35.847	31.921	67.769	17.252	14.979	32.231	0.000	0.000	0.000	53.099	46.901	100.00
6.	Brasli	37.867	37.769	75.636	12.084	12.280	24.364	0.000	0.000	0.000	49.951	50.049	100.00
7.	Dalgaon	31.360	30.290	61.650	18.955	19.395	38.350	0.000	0.000	0.000	50.315	49.685	100.00
8.	Dharara	35.939	34.302	70.242	14.613	15.145	29.758	0.000	0.000	0.000	50.553	49.447	100.00
9.	Hanstari	33.482	34.038	67.519	15.573	16.908	32.481	0.000	0.000	0.000	49.055	50.945	100.00
10.	Jagothi	37.571	36.102	73.672	13.446	12.881	26.328	0.000	0.000	0.000	51.017	48 983	100.00
11.	Kadivan	37.284	33.955	71.238	15.180	13.582	28.762	0.000	0.000	0.000	52.463	47.537	100.00
12.	Karalash	23.119	21.362	44.975	24.492	31.027	55.519	0.000	0.000	0.000	47.611	52.389	100.00
13.	Karasa	37.390	34.539	71.930	14.327	13.743	28.070	0.000	0.000	0.000	51.718	48.282	100.00
14.	Karchhari	2.8.885	27.580	56.465	20.937	22.598	43.535	0.000	0.000	0.000	49.822	50.178	100.00

Contd...

Contd...

15.	Katlah	38.421	37.467	75.888	11.977	12.136	24.112	0.000	0.000	0.000	50.397	49.603	100.00
16.	Khangteri	29.844	28.470	58.314	21.885	19.801	41.686	0.000	0.000	0.000	51.729	48.271	100.00
17.	Kutara	25.670	24.534	50.204	25.398	24.398	49.796	0.000	0.000	0.000	51.068	48.932	100.00
18.	Kuthari	30.015	25.566	55.581	21.342	23.077	44.419	0.000	0.000	0.000	51.357	48.643	100.00
19.	Lower Koti	34.536	32.240	66.776	16.721	16.503	33.223	0.000	0.000	0.000	51.257	48.743	100.00
20.	Munchhara	33.413	32.460	65.873	16.587	17.540	34.127	0.000	0.000	0.000	50.000	50.000	100.00
21.	Puiarali-3	30.120	31.198	61.319	18.580	20.101	8.681	0.000	0.000	0.000	48.700	51.300	100.00
22.	Puiarali-4	30.322	28.160	58.481	21.231	20.288	41.519	0.000	0.000	0.000	51.552	48.448	100.00
23.	Summer Kot	36.342	34.121	70.463	15.359	14.178	29.537	0.000	0.000	0.000	51.701	48.299	100.00
24.	Samoli	35.635	31.998	67.633	16.769	15.598	32.367	0.000	0.000	0.000	52.404	47.596	100.00
25.	Shekhal	24.573	23.390	47.963	22.405	19.777	42.181	0.000	0.000	0.000	51.643	48.357	100.00
26.	Sharontha	30.518	27.735	58.253	21.689	20.058	41.747	0.000	0.000	0.000	0.000	47.793	100.00
27.	Sheel	35.676	34.346	70.022	15.226	14.752	29.978	0.000	0.000	0.000	50.902	49.098	100.00
28.	Rantari (Seema)	27.674	25.797	53.471	17.026	16.698	33.724	0.000	0.000	0.000	50.657	49.343	100.00
29.	Tikkar	33.293	32.214	65.507	17.337	17.157	34.493	0.000	0.000	0.000	50.630	49.370	100.00
	Grand Total	33.274	31.649	64.912	17.148	17.077	34.225	0.000	0.000	0.000	50.825	49.175	100.00

Source: Secretary, Block Development Office, Rohroo.

A total of 44 respondents from the 12 selected panchayats were interviewed, 12 of them were presidents of their respective panchayats, 12 were vice-presidents, 11 were ward members and the rest consisted of officials and some were also members of the Zila Parishad. Out of 44 respondents, 10 were women. As the number of male members in the panchayats was more, a majority of the respondents selected both in the general and the SC categories were male. Among them, 13 were Dalits, of whom five were women (Table 1.2).

Table 1.2

Sex and category-wise distribution of respondents: Rohroo

Sex	*General*	*Scheduled Caste*	*Total*
Male	26 (83.87)	8 (61.54)	34 (77.27)
Female	5 (16.13)	5 (38.46)	10 (22.73)
Total	31 (100)	13 (100)	44 (100)

Note: Figures in parentheses indicate percentages.

Table 1.3

Educational qualification-wise distribution of respondents: Rohroo

Education	*Category*		
	General	*Scheduled Caste*	*Total*
Illiterate	Nil	1 (7.69)	1 (2.27)
Primary	3 (9.68)	2 (15.39)	5 (11.36)
Matric	14 (45.16)	8 (61.54)	22 (50.00)
Plus Two	5 (16.13)	1 (7.69)	6 (13.64)
Graduate	5 (16.13)	0	5 (11.36)
Post-Graduate	4 (12.90)	1 (7.69)	5 (11.36)
Total	31 (100)	13 (100)	44 (100)

Note: Figures in parentheses indicate percentages.

Table 1.3 gives the educational qualification and occupation of the respondents. It shows that majority of the respondents are matriculate (50%), followed by senior secondary (13.64%) and 11.36 per cent each having qualification upto graduation and post-graduation and above. Thus, in HP, Dalits are much better educated than in the other north Indian states selected in our study. It is interesting to note that the percentage of SC respondents who are matriculate are more than those in the general category, but the reverse is true in the case of higher qualifications of graduation and post-graduation. Most of the respondents holding a post at various levels in the panchayats are matriculates and constitute 22 per cent of the total sample. This means that in HP educated persons in comparison with other states in our sample run the panchayats. As Table 1.4 shows the main occupation of the respondents is horticulture, which is followed by business. While the majority are engaged in horticulture, the percentage of SC respondents is more reflecting the larger amount of land held by the upper castes. Fewer number of SC respondents are engaged in business.

Table 1.4

Main occupation-wise distribution of respondents: Rohroo

Main Occupation	*General*	*Scheduled Caste*	*Total*
Business	5 (16.67)	2 (14.30)	7 (15.91)
Agriculture/Horticulture	25 (83.33)	12 (85.70)	37 (84.09)
Total	30 (100)	14 (100)	44 (100)

Note: Figures in parentheses indicate percentages.

Table 1.5 shows a marked difference in the land held by the respondents in the SC and general categories. More than two-thirds of the representatives from general category (68.25%) hold more than 15 bighas of land in comparison to mere 7.69 per cent of SC category. Of the 22.73 per cent of the total respondents, who hold less than 6 bighas of land, 46.16 per cent are from the SCs while only 12.90 per cent are from the general category. Furthermore, no respondent from the SC category holds more than 20 bighas of land, whereas 45.17 per cent representatives from general category possess more than 20 bighas of land. As land is a source of power and prestige in rural areas, it undoubtedly puts the non-Dalits in a commanding position within the village panchayats.

Table 1.5

Landholding size and category-wise distribution of respondents: Rohroo

Landholding Size	*Category*		
	General	*Scheduled Caste*	*Total*
1-5	4 (12.90)	6 (46.16)	10 (22.73)
6-5	2 (6.45)	5 (38.46)	7 (15.91)
11-15	4 (12.90)	1 (7.69)	5 (11.36)
16-20	7 (22.58)	1 (7.69)	8 (18.18)
21-25	5 (16.13)	-	5 (11.36)
Above 25	9 (29.44)	-	9 (20.46)
Total	3 (100)	13 (100)	44 (100)

Note: Figures in parentheses indicate percentages.

Despite being an economically developed area, there is difference in the living conditions of Dalits and non-Dalits. Fewer Dalits live in *pucca* houses with proper sanitation, drinking water and own facilities such as telephone, TV or refrigerator. However, the number of Dalits who have access to these facilities is higher than in other states reflecting the better condition of Dalits in HP.

Sirmaur District: A Profile

In contrast spread over 2,825 sq kms, Sirmaur is a smaller district divided into three sub-divisions, namely, Nahan, Paonta and Rajgarh. Sirmaur as a region is very old being part of a former Hindu princely state and did not experience the impact of colonialism. As a consequence, in contrast to Rohroo, which is close to Shimla town and was an important outpost of the empire, it had a feudal culture and social organization. The caste system with its attendant *jajmani* system was more strongly rooted here. The Brahmins, Rajputs and Kanets (who later acquired Rajput traits) formed the high castes while the Kolis, Dumra or Dumna, Chanals and Chamars and some artisan groups such as Lohars and Badais were accorded a low position.

Sirmaur district has 217 panchayats and 1,311 wards. Of these 24 panchayats from Rajgarh, 12 from Nahan and seven panchayats from Paonta blocks respectively, were selected. Thus, the study was carried out in 43 panchayats of district Sirmaur, which constitute almost 20 per cent of the total panchayats in the districts. All the 43 Sarpanchas of the selected panchayats formed the respondents of the study. As Table 1.6 shows, an equal number of Dalit and non-Dalit male and female Sarpanchas were selected. The Dalits in the sample were from the Koli, Lohar and Dom sub-castes, who form a predominant section among the Dalits in these panchayats.

Table 1.6

Gender, caste and development block-wise distribution of leaders: Sirmaur

Gender	*Caste*	*Blocks*			
		Rajgarh	*Sangrah*	*Paonta*	*Total*
Male	*Non-Dalit*				
	Rajput	6	3	-	9
	Brahman	-	1	-	1
	Dalit				
	Koli	6	2	-	8
	OBC	-	-	2	2
Female	*Non-Dalit*				
	Rajput	4	3	-	7
	Brahman	2	-	-	2
	Dalit				
	Koli	4	3	2	9
	Lohar	1	-	-	1
	Dom	1	-	-	1
	OBC	-	-	3	3
Total		24	12	7	43

Tables 1.7 to 1.10 provide the age, educational background, landownership pattern and income of the respondents. They show the rise of relatively younger and better-educated Dalit Sarpanchas - both male and female - though there are five Dalit Sarpanchas above the age of 45. A large number of the Dalit Sarpanchas are within the age group of 25-44. There is no non-Dalit male or female Sarpanch in the age group of 20-24, whereas, there are two Dalit female Sarpanchas. The 73rd Constitutional Amendment has led to the entry of younger Dalits, particularly women, into the panchayats. Dalit Sarpanchas - both male and female are as well educated as non-Dalit Sarpanchas. But there is no Dalit Sarpanch who has been able to complete graduation. However, some of the male Dalit respondents have been able to obtain a diploma in health care, carpentry and tailoring. Thus, education appears to be an enabling factor for Dalit leadership in general and women in particular. However, the educational levels of the respondents are not as high as in Rohroo block where a larger number of them have been able to enter higher education.

Table 1.7

Age-wise distribution of leaders: Sirmaur

Gender	*Caste*	*Age (in years)*							
		20-24	*25-29*	*30-34*	*35-39*	*40-44*	*45-49*	*50+*	*Total*
Male	Non-Dalit	-	-	5	1	2	1	1	10
	Dalit	-	2	-	2	1	3	2	10
Female	Non-Dalit	-	1	1	2	3	1	1	9
	Dalit	2	4	2	3	2	-	1	14
Total		2	8	8	8	8	5	5	43

Table 1.8

Educational qualification-wise distribution of leaders: Sirmaur

Gender	Caste	Education						
		Nil	Primary	Middle	Matric	10+2	BA	Total
Male	Non-Dalit	1	1	2	5	-	1	10
	Dalit	-	1	3	5	1	-	10
Female	Non-Dalit	-	5	1	2	1	-	9
	Dalit	1	3	3	6.	1	-	14
Total		2	10	8	17	3	1	43

Table 1.9

Landownership-wise distribution of leaders: Sirmaur

Gender	Caste	Total Land					
		Up to 20	21-40	41-60	61-80	81+	Total
Male	Non-Dalit	5	2	2	1	-	10
	Dalit	8	2	-	-	-	10
Female	Non-Dalit	-	5	2	2	-	9
	Dalit	8	6	-	-	-	14
Total		21	15	4	3	-	43

Table 1.10

Income-wise distribution of leaders: Sirmaur

Gender	Caste	Income (in Rs per month)							
		Up to 1000	1001-2000	2001-3000	3001-4000	4001-5000	5001-6000	6001 +	Total
Male	Non-Dalit	1	4	-	1	1	2	1	10
	Dalit	4	2	1	1	-	-	2	10
Female	Non-Dalit	1	1	1	1	2	2	1	9
	Dalit	-	8	2	1	-	1	2	14
Total		6	15	4	4	3	4	6	43

But Tables 1.9 and 1.10 show that Dalits as in Rohroo are at a disadvantage, so far as landownership and income are concerned. Dalits own small plots ranging between 20 and 40 bighas and no Dalit owns plots above 40 bighas, whereas seven non-Dalits own plots, which are above 40 bighas. In terms of income, the largest number of respondents (Dalit and non-Dalit) are concentrated in the income category of Rs. 1,000-2,000, which points to the backwardness of the region. Less non-Dalits fall into the category lower than this and there are only three Dalits earning more than Rs. 4,000 a month and above compared to 10 non-Dalits. Thus, non-Dalits have a higher income than Dalits perhaps due to the landownership differentials. Regarding housing and other facilities, such as drinking water and sanitation, although both Dalit and non-Dalit respondents owned houses but the houses of the non-Dalits were much bigger and better built and had better sanitation facilities such as wet latrines with septic tank. However, all the respondents had access to tap water. Most respondents did not own any means of transport. Only two Dalit respondents owned a scooter, one owned a motor cycle, one a truck but none had a car. Three non-Dalits owned a car or van whereas two owned a scooter and motorcycle.

Thus, we find that there are differences between the selected blocks in Shimla and Sirmaur districts: Dalits are better educated and better off in the former than in the latter. However, despite this, on many counts such as landownership and income, in both the districts, the non-Dalit leadership is better placed than the Dalit leadership. This gives the former, as we shall see, a predominant position in village society as well as an advantage in the panchayats.

Much social change has taken place in the state, which has also altered the context in which panchayats function. For example, earlier, Dalits were expected to keep a social distance and there is also recorded history indicating untouchability existing earlier. The major difference now is that it is not practised in the public sphere and has been restricted to the private sphere only. In the panchayats, in Sirmaur block, the survey showed that Dalits are allowed entry into non-Dalit houses except in some parts, which the latter would like to keep separate even today. These are the kitchen and the upper storey of the houses, which in this region is the place of worship where all religious texts and idols are kept. Thus, notions of purity and pollution based on Hindu religion still exist but are restricted to the private spheres. Similarly, there are restrictions on inter-dining. But this is not practised in other public places, such as, schools, where children eat together and religious places Dalits are allowed freely to participate in religious congregations. None of the respondents mentioned any instance of derogatory behaviour against them. Most important, there are few restrictions on use of common property resources such as cremation grounds, forest resources, public roads, access to shops, services of barbers, entry to hotels etc. This means that Dalits who are elected can enter into panchayat bhawans and participate in meetings though the existing power structure may not allow them to participate in decision-making. However, this does not mean that caste-based discrimination has totally disappeared. Rather, more subtle and newer forms are used. Pressure tactics are often used by the upper castes to get certain favours or make decisions which are favourable to them. The brunt of these tactics is felt by the lower castes – both male and female. There is also a feeling expressed by some non-Dalit respondents that in the prevailing scenario Dalits who are numerically large in some regions are asserting and acquiring greater political space, leaving little for others. Thus, Dalits face problems today as much because of their economic and political powerlessness as their social and cultural background and this impacts, as we shall see later, on the functioning of panchayats.

Dalit Leadership in Rohroo and Sirmaur District Panchayats

Dalit Leadership in Rohroo Panchayat

An important reason for the failure of Dalit representatives to play an effective role is the lack of awareness and knowledge about reservation provided in the new panchayats. Table 1.11 gives the level of awareness and satisfaction of respondents with the reservation system. In Rohroo, 47.73 per cent of the total representatives were aware of reservation to some extent but 22.72 per cent were not aware at all. Dalit representatives showed greater awareness than the general category representatives, which is a reflection of rising political and social consciousness and a desire for a share in power and decision-making at the local level. Only 15.38 per cent of the Dalit representatives as against 25.81 per cent of the general category representatives had no knowledge of the existence of reservations. Further, the survey revealed that 40 per cent of the female respondents were not aware of the reservation system in comparison to 17.64 per cent males.

Table 1.11

Category-wise extent of awareness about reservation system: Rohroo

Extent of awareness about reservation system	*Category*		
	General	*Scheduled Caste*	*Total*
To large extent	9 (29.03)	4 (30.71)	13 (29.55)
To some extent	14 (45.16)	7 (53.85)	21 (47.73)
Not at all	8 (25.81)	2 (15.38)	10 (22.72)
Total	31 (100)	13 (100)	44 (100)

Note: Figures in parentheses indicate percentages.

Table 1.12

Reservation system and satisfaction level: Rohroo

Satisfaction level	*Category*		
	General	*Scheduled Caste*	*Total*
Satisfied	24 (77.42)	12 (92.31)	36 (81.82)
Not Satisfied	7 (22.58)	1 (7.69)	8 (18.18)
Total	31 (100)	13 (100)	44 (100)

Note: Figures in parentheses indicate percentages.

Table 1.12 shows that 81.82 per cent were satisfied with the reservation policy but 18.18 per cent expressed their dissatisfaction with it. Except for one, all Dalit representatives are fully satisfied with the reservation policy and feel that it would provide them upward mobility and influence at the local level.

Table 1.13

Reservation for women: Rohroo

Response	*Category*								
	General			*Scheduled Caste*			*Grand Total*		
	Male	*Female*	*Total*	*Male*	*Female*	*Total*	*Male*	*Female*	*Total*
Yes	18 (96.23)	5 (100)	23 (74.19)	8 (100)	5 (100)	13 (100)	26 (76.47)	10 (100)	36 (81.82)
No	8 (30.77)	- -	8 (25.81)	- -	- -	- -	8 (23.53)	- -	8 (18.18)
Total	26 (100)	5 (100)	31 (100)	8 (100)	5 (100)	13 (100)	34 (100)	10 (100)	44 (100)

Note: Figures in parentheses indicate percentages.

Table 1.13 shows that there is no opposition to reservation for women among the representatives, which is a reflection of the position women have traditionally occupied in the Himachali society. It is evident from the table that more than four-fifths of the total respondents (81.82%) have favoured the reservation for women in PRIs. Not surprisingly, all the female respondents, irrespective of their caste, have favoured reservation for women in PRIs, in comparison to 76.47 per cent male respondents. All the male respondents from the SC category favoured reservation for women.

Reservation policy can be successfully implemented only when the large majority of the non-Dalits in a region give up their belief in the caste system and the practice of untouchability in the social sphere and are prepared to share power at the local level with Dalits. The conflict and violence, even the beheading of successful Dalit representatives, witnessed in panchayat elections in Tamil Nadu, is a good example of the opposition to Dalits entering the panchayats by the dominant landowning castes. On the contrary, in Rohroo, we find, as Table 1.14 also shows, that 75 per cent of the respondents do not believe in the caste system, though the percentage is higher among the Dalit (84.62%) than the non-Dalit respondents (70.97%). But, at least 29.03 per cent of the general category respondents did profess belief in the caste system.

Table 1.14

Belief in caste system: Rohroo

Category-wise Response	*Caste*		
	General	*Scheduled Caste*	*Total*
Yes	9 (29.03)	2 (15.38)	11 (25.00)
No	22 (70.97)	11 (84.62)	33 (75.00)
Total	31 (100)	13 (100)	44 (100)

Note: Figures in parentheses indicate percentages.

Table 1.15

Eradicating caste barriers through literacy: Rohroo

Response	*Category*		
	General	*Scheduled Caste*	*Total*
Yes	25 (80.65)	13 (100)	38 (86.36)
No	6 (19.35)	-	33 (13.64)
Total	31 (100)	13 (100)	44 (100)

Note: Figures in parentheses indicate percentages.

Table 1.16

Practice of untouchability: Rohroo

Response	*Category*		
	General	*Scheduled Caste*	*Total*
Yes	25 (80.65)	13 (100)	38 (86.36)
No	6 (19.25)	-	6 (13.64)
Total	31 (100)	13 (100)	44 (100)

Note: Figures in parentheses indicate percentages.

Table 1.15 shows that a large majority of respondents (86.36%), including all Dalit respondents, believe that eradication of the caste system is possible through literacy. Dalits in recent years have viewed education as the ladder for upward mobility and that the provision of reservation in educational institutions makes employment in the government possible. As they do not own land or other assets, education has emerged as the path of socio-economic and political mobility. However, as Table 1.16 reveals, at the same time, as much as 80.65 per cent of the general category respondents and 100 per cent of the Dalit respondents admitted that untouchability is still practised in the area. Only 13.64 per cent of the total respondents felt that it was not practised. As we shall see later, this has an impact on the functioning of the panchayats here.

Functioning of Dalit Leaders in the Panchayats

Reservation provides Dalits a position within the new panchayats but is not a guarantee that they will be able to effectively participate in the decision-making process. It is the level of participation of Dalit leaders that will determine the success of the reservation policy. Traditionally, the upper castes were dominant at the grassroots level and a person from lower caste was rarely given an opportunity to head the PRIs. It was only after the 73rd Constitutional Amendment Act in which provision for reservation of seats to weaker sections of the society was made. After the implementation of new PRI system, two elections, i.e., in 1995 and 2000, have been held to these bodies in HP.

Responses of the sample respondents presented in Table 1.17 reveal that majority of them (70.45%) feel that upper castes no longer control the functioning of the PRIs. As much as 76.92 per cent of the Dalit and 67.74 per cent of the non-Dalit respondents felt that the upper castes no longer have influence on their functioning. But Table 1.18 shows that almost 66 per cent of the sample respondents felt that functioning of Dalit representatives in PRIs is still influenced by higher caste representatives as well as higher caste people of that area. But a majority of the Dalit respondents do not agree with this. We seem to be witnessing a phase of transition from control by the upper castes to greater sharing of power and influence with the Dalits. Reservations have aided this process by making it faster. This is evident from the next two tables (1.19 and 1.20) which show that Dalits are gaining cooperation and due respect from the higher castes in the panchayats.

Table 1.17

Influence of upper castes in PRIs: Rohroo

Response	*Category*		
	General	*Scheduled Caste*	*Total*
Yes	10 (32.26)	3 (23.08)	13 (29.55)
No	21 (67.74)	10 (76.92)	31 (70.45)
Total	31 (100)	13 (100)	44 (100)

Note: Figures in parentheses indicate percentages.

Table 1.18

Pressure of higher castes on Dalit representatives: Rohroo

Response	*Category*								
	General			*Scheduled Caste*			*Grand Total*		
	Male	*Female*	*Total*	*Male*	*Female*	*Total*	*Male*	*Female*	*Total*
Yes	19 (73.08)	4 (80)	23 (74.19)	4 (50)	2 (40)	6 (46.15)	23 (67.15)	6 (60)	29 (65.91)
No	7 (26.92)	1 (20)	8 (25.81)	4 (50)	3 (60)	7 (53.85)	11 (32.35)	4 (40)	15 (34.09)
Total	26 (100)	5 (100)	31 (100)	8 (100)	5 (100)	13 (100)	34 (100)	10 (100)	44 (100)

Note: Figures in parentheses indicate percentages.

Table 1.19

Role of Dalits in decision-making: Rohroo

Response	Category								
	General			Scheduled Caste			Grand Total		
	Male	Female	Total	Male	Female	Total	Male	Female	Total
Yes	26 (100)	5 (100)	31 (100)	8 (100)	5 (100)	13 (100)	34 (100)	10 (100)	44 (100)
No	-	-	-	-	-	-	-	-	-
Total	26 (100)	5 (100)	31 (100)	8 (100)	5 (100)	13 (100)	34 (100)	10 (100)	44 (100)

Note: Figures in parentheses indicate percentages.

Table 1.20

Efficiency of Dalit representatives: Rohroo

Response	Category								
	General			Scheduled Caste			Grand Total		
	Male	Female	Total	Male	Female	Total	Male	Female	Total
Yes	18 (69.23)	5 (100)	23 (74.19)	8 (100)	4 (80)	12 (92.31)	26 (76.47)	9 (90)	35 (79.55)
No	8 (30.77)	- -	8 (25.81)	- -	1 (20)	1 (7.69)	8 (23.53)	1 (10)	9 (20.45)
Total	26 (100)	5 (100)	31 (100)	8 (100)	5 (100)	13 (100)	34 (100)	10 (100)	44 (100)

Note: Figures in parentheses indicate percentages.

Against this background, it is not surprising to see Dalits to be included in the decision-making process in the panchayats. Decision-making is one of the most important functions of every representative of PRIs. It requires capability of representatives of PRIs in order to utilize limited resources for developmental works in their respective area. Table 1.19 reveals that all respondents, irrespective of their sex and category, agree that Dalit representatives take all decisions on their own and are not influenced by the higher caste representative in this regard. Moreover, slightly more than three-fourths of respondents feel that Dalit representatives are quite efficient in discharging various duties as public representatives (Table 1.20). Further, nearly three-fourths of general category respondents are satisfied with the working of Dalit representatives as against 90 per cent SC respondents. Table 1.21 indicates that an overwhelming majority (93.18%) of the respondents point to good coordination between the Dalit and non-Dalit women representatives. All women representatives, irrespective of caste, have subscribed to this view. Similarly, all the male representatives from the SC category also believe that there is a proper cooperation between the Dalit and non-Dalit women representatives as against 88.46 per cent from general category.

Table 1.21

Cooperation between Dalit and non-Dalit women representatives: Rohroo

Response	*Category*								
	General			*Scheduled Caste*			*Grand Total*		
	Male	*Female*	*Total*	*Male*	*Female*	*Total*	*Male*	*Female*	*Total*
Yes	23	5	28	8	5	13	31	10	41
	(88.46)	(100)	(90.32)	(100)	(100)	(100)	(91.18)	(100)	(93.18)
No	3	-	3	-	-	-	3	-	3
	(11.54)	-	(9.68)	-	-	-	(8.82)	-	(6.82)
Total	26	5	31	8	5	13	34	10	44
	(100)	(100)	(100)	(100)	(100)	(100)	(100)	(100)	(100)

Note: Figures in parentheses indicate percentages.

Following the 73rd amendment, women have started playing an important role in the functioning of the panchayats. Table 1.22 shows that the respondents feel that women, including Dalit women, have been able to play an effective role in the functioning of PRIs. All the female representatives, irrespective of their caste, consider their representation in the PRIs very effective as against 67.65 per cent male representatives. Male representatives, who consider women's representation in the working of PRIs effective, was higher in the SC category (87.50%) in comparison to general category (61.54%). Table 1.23 reveals that all the female representatives, irrespective of their caste, consider Dalit women representatives equally effective in the working of PRIs as their counterparts. And 87.5 per cent male representatives from the SC category and 53.85 per cent from general category believe that Dalit women representatives are equally effective in the

Table 1.22

Effectiveness of women representatives: Rohroo

Response	*Category*								
	General			*Scheduled Caste*			*Grand Total*		
	Male	*Female*	*Total*	*Male*	*Female*	*Total*	*Male*	*Female*	*Total*
Yes	16	5	21	7	5	12	23	10	33
	(61.54)	(100)	(67.74)	(87.5)	(100)	(92.31)	(67.65)	(100)	(75)
No	10	-	10	1	-	1	11	-	11
	(38.46)	-	(32.26)	(12.5)	-	(7.69)	(32.35)	-	(25)
Total	26	5	31	8	5	13	34	10	44
	(100)	(100)	(100)	(100)	(100)	(100)	(100)	(100)	(100)

Note: Figures in parentheses indicate percentages.

Table 1.23

Effectiveness of Dalit women representatives: Rohroo

Response	*Category*								
	General			*Scheduled Caste*			*Grand Total*		
	Male	*Female*	*Total*	*Male*	*Female*	*Total*	*Male*	*Female*	*Total*
Yes	14	5	19	7	5	12	21	10	31
	(53.85)	(100)	(61.29)	(87.5)	(100)	(92.31)	(61.76)	(100)	(70.45)
No	12	-	12	1	-	1	13	-	13
	(46.15)	-	(38.71)	(12.5)	-	(7.69)	(38.24)	-	(29.55)
Total	26	5	31	8	5	13	34	10	44
	(100)	(100)	(100)	(100)	(100)	(100)	(100)	(100)	(100)

Note: Figures in parentheses indicate percentages.

functioning of PRIs. Moreover, Table 1.24 shows that almost four-fifths of the sampled respondents hold that there is active involvement of women representatives in the decision-making process. Interestingly, all the female respondents, irrespective of their caste, feel that they have a greater say in decision-making in the PRIs. Number of male respondents who subscribe to this view are more in the SC category (87.50%) than in the general category (69.23%).

Table 1.24

Role of women in decision-making: Rohroo

Response	*Category*								
	General			*Scheduled Caste*			*Grand Total*		
	Male	*Female*	*Total*	*Male*	*Female*	*Total*	*Male*	*Female*	*Total*
Yes	18	5	23	7	5	12	25	10	35
	(69.23)	(100)	(74.19)	(87.5)	(100)	(92.31)	(73.53)	(100)	(79.55)
No	8	-	8	1	-	1	9	-	9
	(30.77)	-	(25.81)	(12.5)	-	(7.69)	(26.47)	-	(20.45)
Total	26	5	31	8	5	13	34	10	44
	(100)	(100)	(100)	(100)	(100)	(100)	(100)	(100)	(100)

Note: Figures in parentheses indicate percentages.

Granting of powers and functions and the provision of adequate funds for panchayats is essential, if they are to carry out developmental tasks. Since panchayats do not generate adequate resources at their own level, they depend for financial support on the government. Table 1.25 reveals that 86.36 per cent PRI representatives find that the available funds are insufficient. Respondents in the general category are more aware of this shortcoming than the Dalit respondents. Under the new PRI system, panchayats have been granted additional powers and functions but in real sense these powers and functions are yet to be realized by the PRI functionaries due to bureaucratic hurdles and lack of political will at higher level. Table 1.26 highlights that 93.18 per cent of the respondents, more of them from the general category, feel that more powers should be vested with PRIs.

Table 1.25

Availability of funds for developmental projects: Rohroo

Response	Category								
	General			Scheduled Caste			Grand Total		
	Male	Female	Total	Male	Female	Total	Male	Female	Total
Yes	2	1	3	2	1	3	4	2	6
	(7.67)	(20)	(9.68)	(25)	(20)	(23.08)	(11.76)	(20)	(13.64)
No	24	4	28	6	4	10	30	8	38
	(92.31)	(80)	(90.32)	(75)	(80)	(76.92)	(88.24)	(80)	(86.36)
Total	26	5	31	8	5	13	34	10	44
	(100)	(100)	(100)	(100)	(100)	(100)	(100)	(100)	(100)

Note: Figures in parentheses indicate percentages.

Table 1.26

Increasing the powers of PRIs: Rohroo

Response	Category								
	General			Scheduled Caste			Grand Total		
	Male	Female	Total	Male	Female	Total	Male	Female	Total
Yes	24	5	29	7	5	12	31	10	41
	(93.18)	(92.31)	(100)	(93.55)	(87.5)	(100)	(92.31)	(91.18)	(100)
No	2	-	2	1	-	1	3	-	3
	(7.69)	-	(6.45)	(12.5)	-	(7.69)	(8.82)	-	(6.82)
Total	26	5	31	8	5	13	34	10	44
	(100)	(100)	(100)	(100)	(100)	(100)	(100)	(100)	(100)

Note: Figures in parentheses indicate percentages.

Under the new PRI system, various types of incentives are being provided to Dalits and all women in particular. In this regard, the representatives were asked whether Dalits are really getting benefits under the new PRIs schemes. Analysis of Table 1.27 reveals that 86.36 per cent, more of them being women, feel that Dalits are being benefited under the new PRI schemes.

A higher number of Dalit respondents agreed that they are gaining substantial benefits from the new panchayat system.

Table 1.27

Benefits to Dalits through new PRI system: Rohroo

Response	*Category*								
	General			*Scheduled Caste*			*Grand Total*		
	Male	*Female*	*Total*	*Male*	*Female*	*Total*	*Male*	*Female*	*Total*
Yes	22 (84.62)	4 (80)	26 (83.87)	7 (87.5)	5 (100)	12 (92.31)	29 (85.29)	9 (90)	38 (86.36)
No	4 (15.38)	1 (20)	5 (16.13)	1 (12.5)	- -	1 (7.69)	5 (14.71)	1 (10)	6 (13.64)
Total	26 (100)	5 (100)	31 (100)	8 (100)	5 (100)	13 (100)	34 (100)	10 (100)	44 (100)

Note: Figures in parentheses indicate percentages.

Table 1.28

Coordination between government official and PRI representative: Sex and category-wise: Rohroo

Response	*Category*								
	General			*Scheduled Caste*			*Grand Total*		
	Male	*Female*	*Total*	*Male*	*Female*	*Total*	*Male*	*Female*	*Total*
Yes	21 (80.77)	5 (100)	25 (83.87)	8 (100)	5 (100)	13 (100)	29 (85.29)	10 (100)	39 (88.64)
No	5 (19.23)	- -	5 (16.13)	- -	- -	- -	5 (14.71)	- -	44 (100)
Total	26 (100)	5 (100)	31 (100)	8 (100)	5 (100)	13 (100)	34 (100)	10 (100)	44 (100)

Note: Figures in parentheses indicate percentages.

Cooperation from government officials engaged in the functioning is crucial for the smooth and vibrant functioning of PRIs. A majority of respondents felt that there was adequate coordination and cooperation between the panchayats and the government officials (Table 1.28). Also more than two-thirds of the respondents did not find any interference by the government in the day-to-day functioning of the panchayats (Table 1.29).

Table 1.29

Interference in the working of PRI by state government: Sex and category-wise: Rohroo

Response	Category								
	General			Scheduled Caste			Grand Total		
	Male	Female	Total	Male	Female	Total	Male	Female	Total
Yes	11	1	12	2	-	2	13	1	14
	(42.31)	(20)	(38.71)	(25)	-	(15.30)	(38.24)	(10)	(31.82)
No	15	4	19	6	5	11	21	9	30
	(57.69)	(80)	(61.29)	(75)	(100)	(84.62)	(61.76)	(90)	(68.18)
Total	26	5	31	8	5	13	34	10	44
	(100)	(100)	(100)	(100)	(100)	(100)	(100)	(100)	(100)

Note: Figures in parentheses indicate percentages.

Dalit Leadership in Sirmaur Panchayats

Table 1.30 shows that all respondents are aware of the new Panchayat Act and its provisions. However, Dalits, both male and female, have greater knowledge about them. Most of them are also aware of the 73rd Constitutional Amendment Act. A major reason is that the Dalits in the area are highly conscious of their rights and have in recent years become assertive. On being questioned they showed knowledge about various programmes at the panchayat level such as housing, self-employment opportunities, loans etc., though they are not very much conversant with the details of the programmes. Apart from the low level of education in some cases, this is mainly because they are not given training or any orientation on being elected to the panchayat. Table 1.31 reveals that male respondents, both Dalits and non-Dalits, have a good understanding of the powers and functions of the panchayats. But non-Dalit and to a lesser extent Dalit females are not as

Table 1.30

Awareness of new panchayat act and its provisions: Sirmaur

Gender	*Caste*	*Not at all*	*To some extent*	*Almost complete*	*Total*
Male	Non-Dalit	-	3	7	18
	Dalit	-	1	9	10
Female	Non-Dalit	1	6	2	9
	Dalit	1	6	7	14
Total		2	16	25	43

Table 1.31

Awareness of panchayat functions and powers: Sirmaur

Gender	*Caste*	*To some extent*	*Almost complete*	*Total*
Male	Non-Dalit	2	8	10
	Dalit	1	9	10
Female	Non-Dalit	6	3	9
	Dalit	8	6	14
Total		17	27	43

Table 1.32

Perception about the existing reservation policy provisions: Sirmaur

Gender	*Caste*	*Enough to meet the needs*	*Need to add more*	*Total*
Male	Non-Dalit	9	1	10
	Dalit	8	2	10
Female	Non-Dalit	9	-	9
	Dalit	12	2	14
Total		38	5	43

knowledgeable. Women elected to the panchayat have yet to acquire better awareness of the powers given to panchayats and the role they are expected to play at the local level. As Table 1.32 unveils the large majority of respondents felt that the existing reservation policy is worthwhile, they are satisfied and only a small number felt that the government needs to do more to help the Dalits.

Table 1.33
Awareness of role as a pradhan: Sirmaur

Gender	*Caste*	*Not at all*	*To some extent*	*Almost complete*	*Total*
Male	Non-Dalit	-	-	10	10
	Dalit	-	1	9	10
Female	Non-Dalit	2	3	4	9
	Dalit	2	5	7	14
Total		4	9	30	43

Table 1.34
Knowledge about panchayat's financial sources and position: Sirmaur

Gender	*Caste*	*To some extent*	*Almost complete*	*Total*
Male	Non-Dalit	3	7	10
	Dalit	-	10	10
Female	Non-Dalit	3	6	9
	Dalit	5	9	14
Total		11	32	43

Table 1.33 discloses that 30 out of 43 respondents showed awareness of their role as Pradhans and felt it was an important post they occupied. But this awareness was higher among men than women in the case of both Dalits and non-Dalits, indicating that women had yet to realize the importance of the post they were holding. Table 1.34 shows that while all respondents were keenly aware, Dalits knew more about the financial powers and functioning of the panchayats than the non-Dalits. It indicates that Dalits were taking more interest in the functioning of the panchayats, perhaps because of large number of programmes for weaker sections. This was true of the women as well. They even knew that the financial position of most panchayats was not sound. The knowledge also pertains to the expenditure incurred on the ongoing projects and what is to be done in the coming times. But, here also, the panchayat leadership is not very clear.

Table 1.35

Suggestions to improve the lot of Dalits by panchayat: Sirmaur

Suggestions	*Non-Dalit*		*Dalit*		*Total*
	M	*F*	*M*	*F*	
Employment opportunities in the villages	5	3	6	6	20
Infra-structure development	1	3	2	5	11
Provision of basic services	2	3	2	1	8
Streamlining of the government programmes	1	2	2	3	8
Economically weak Dalits be given priority over others	1	-	1	2	4
Total	10	11	13	16	50*

* Number increases due to multiple reasons.

The general conditions of the Dalits are not very encouraging. The prevailing high rate of unemployment among the youth, rising prices and other difficulties in living a normal life make the existence of common people difficult, especially the Dalits. One of the alternatives for the improvement of the lot of Dalits is the creation of employment opportunities in the villages. Since the creation of employment opportunities depends upon infrastructure development, some of the leaders, as depicted in Table 1.35, feel that there is need for such activities, which would lead to further creation of employment opportunities. The others refer to streamlining of the government programmes on the one hand and priority to Dalits over the others on the other, being the two important suggestions. Although, the data do not indicate large differences between the responses of non-Dalits and Dalits, the latter was to be found more vocal in this context. Since the government programmes do not reach the needy, the streamlining is required with immediate effect. In fact, a recent study of minorities in Himachal Pradesh emphasized on the need to take the programmes to the villages, as these do not reach them (Sharma and Singh, 2002). The above suggestions, therefore, are important as these provide direct benefits to the Dalits.

Table 1.36

Participation in panchayat activities: Sirmaur

Gender	*Caste*	*Yes*	*No*	*Total*
Male	Non-Dalit	10	-	10
	Dalit	10	-	10
Female	Non-Dalit	9	-	9
	Dalit	10	4	14
Total		39	4	43

Table 1.37

Nature of participation in panchayat activities: Sirmaur

Gender	*Caste*	*Election canvassing*	*All kinds of activities*	*Total*
Male	Non-Dalit	1	9	10
	Dalit	1	9	10
Female	Non-Dalit	1	8	9
	Dalit	2	12	14
Total		5	38	43

Table 1.38

Level and nature of participation: Sirmaur

Activities	*Frequency*	*%age*
Canvassing during all elections	34	19.76
All types of political activities	34	19.76
Participation in the organization of demonstrations	25	14.53
Mobilization of membership of party	30	17.44
Helping the people in their problems	15	8.72
Representing the interests of the Dalits	34	19.76
Total	172	100.00

Table 1.39

Determinants of participation: Sirmaur

Gender	*Caste*	*Response*					
		No/NA	*Own will*	*Party*	*Friends*	*Any Other*	*Total*
Male	Non-Dalit	-	3	3	2	2	10
	Dalit	-	9	1	1	-	11
Female	Non-Dalit	-	9	-	2	-	11
	Dalit	4	7	1	3	1	16
Total		4	28	5	8	3	48*

*Number increases more than 43 due to multiple responses.

Social change has taken place in Sirmaur in the post-independence period leading to greater participation by Dalits. Table 1.36 shows high level of participation in the panchayats by the Dalits in Sirmaur block. Some female Dalit respondents, however, felt that they were not given a chance to participate. Table 1.37 reveals that the large majority of both the non-Dalit and Dalit leaders participate in all types of political activities. Out of 43 respondents, 38 agreed with this. Table 1.38 shows that the respondents participate in a number of activities from the level of Gram Panchayat, Panchayat Samiti, Zila Parishad, assembly elections, parliamentary elections, etc. These activities include participation in the campaigns in all types of elections held in their respective constituencies. They participate in all sorts of activities as and when called upon by the political party to which they belong. Some of the leaders specifically refer to mobilization of membership for the party, helping the people to make their public image and look into the interests of the Dalits or those who are not in a position to help themselves. It may be mentioned here that there are no caste differences observed in the participation in various activities. However, at the level of gender, the data indicate that the participation of women, both

Dalit and non-Dalits, is relatively less than that of men. Yet, at the same time, the participation in various types of activities of the leadership is determined by a number of factors (Table 1.39). A number of respondents participate in accordance with their own will and not under any type of coercion or pressure but a number of them are guided by their friends and party considerations. Among the other reasons mentioned is membership of Mahila Mandal.

The participation of women in general and Dalit women in particular had been a controversial matter. However, there is considerable change taking place in the society that has also opened up new avenues for women in various spheres of social, economic and even political life. The participation of women in general and Dalit women in particular has increased manifold even in political activities. Their participation at the grassroots leadership circle enjoys positive appreciation. This is evident from the data presented in Table 1.40.

Table 1.40

Behaviour towards participation of Dalit women: Sirmaur

Gender and Caste	*Response of Leadership*		
	Positive	*Indifferent/NA*	*Total*
Non-Dalit men	10	-	10
Dalit men	10	-	10
Non-Dalit women	9	-	9
Dalit women	10	4	14
Total	39	4	43

While there are problems confronted by the panchayat leadership during elections, there are also a number of supporting factors helping the leadership to occupy the central position in the village power structure (Table 1.41). A number of the respondents refer to reservation policy that has helped the Dalits, particularly Dalit women, to win elections. Among other factors cited political affiliations, good reputation and family support matter a lot. It may also be noted that the Dalit women have been more vocal than the others in expressing themselves and one-third of them consider that good reputation in the community is important to come to power.

Table 1.41

Supporting factors in Dalits' coming to power: Sirmaur

Problems	*Non-Dalit*		*Dalit*		*Total*
	M	*F*	*M*	*F*	
Reservation of seats	1	2	1	6	10
Political affiliation	2	2	1	5	10
Support of the family members	2	-	-	7	9
Good reputation in the community	2	1	2	9	14
Total	7	5	4	27	43

Table 1.42

Frequency of participation in panchayat activities: Sirmaur

Gender	*Caste*	*Regular*	*Sometimes*	*Rare*	*Total*
Dalit by non-Dalits					
Male	Dalit	8	2	-	10
Female	Dalit	11	2	1	14
Non-Dalits by Dalits					
Male	Non-Dalit	8	2	-	10
Female	Non-Dalit	9	-	-	9
Total		36	6	1	43

Table 1.42 shows that Dalit leaders are fairly regular in attending panchayat meetings and other activities. Meetings are generally held once a month and fixed in consultation with the Block Development Officer concerned. The issues discussed at these meetings pertain to the overall development of the village.

Members take stock of the ongoing construction and developmental activities, expenditure occurred on various activities, welfare measures, education, health and environmental issues. All the respondents take part in the decision-making process. The views of the Pradhan and Up-Pradhan are given due consideration but decisions are taken by the majority and dissension, if any, is noted. But Dalits are not very vocal in discussing the problems and issues concerning their villages. They, therefore, do not come out with some of the most critical issues they confront at the village level.

Table 1.43

Major hindrances in the working of leadership: Sirmaur

Hindrances	*Non-Dalit*		*Dalit*		*Total*
	M	*F*	*M*	*F*	
Reservation of seats	1	2	1	6	10
Lack of education	4	6	4	-	11
Existing feudal nature of social structure	2	2	6	6	16
Weak economic status of the leaders	1	-	2	2	5
Lack of support from one's own community	3	-	1	-	4
Lack of family support especially for the women leaders	-	-	3	-	3
No problem	2	1	-	6	9
Total	12	9	13	14	48*

*Number increases due to multiple reasons.

Despite signs of successful working of Dalit leadership at the grassroots level, the scope for further improvements always remains. They find that it is not always smooth sailing as there are many hindrances. While the lack of education and lack of support from one's own community are cited as major hindrances by the non-Dalit male and female leaders, the continuity of feudal structure is referred to by the Dalit male and female leaders as the major problem (Table 1.43). In the case of women leaders, it has been found that they are very active and tend to participate in all the activities. But there is a lack of support for them from their own families. This not only curbs their free participation but also their personal growth as leaders and the growth of grassroots democracy.

Table 1.44

Relationships between Pradhan and Up-Pradhan: Sirmaur

Gender	*Caste*	*Relationship*			
		Very Good	*Good*	*Indifferent*	*Total*
Male	Non-Dalit	8	1	1	10
	Dalit	8	2	-	10
Female	Non-Dalit	6	3	-	9
	Dalit	7	5	2	14
Total		29	11	3	43

Table 1.45

Perceived consequences of unfavourable relations on the community and its development: Sirmaur

Gender	*Caste*	*Yes*	*No*	*Total*
Male	Non-Dalit	9	1	10
	Dalit	10	-	10
Female	Non-Dalit	7	2	9
	Dalit	10	4	14
Total		36	7	43

Table 1.46

Perceived consequences-unfavourable relations with government on the community and its development: Sirmaur

Gender	*Caste*	*Yes*	*No*	*Total*
Male	Non-Dalit	8	2	10
	Dalit	9	1	10
Female	Non-Dalit	9	-	9
	Dalit	11	3	14
Total		37	6	43

Both the Dalit and non-Dalit Pradhans, by and large, have good relationships with their Up-Pradhans as well as the ward members (Table 1.44). One of the reasons being that they are of the same party. But, generally, the high caste resent the low caste or the Dalit Pradhan over various issues. The majority of the panchayat leaders also realize that unfavourable relationship with the Dalit leadership is not good for the community as a whole (Table 1.45). The basic reason cited by them is that such an environment further vitiates the entire system and disrupts the functioning. Mostly non-Dalit and Dalit male leaders are of this view. Similarly, all the Dalit and non-Dalit leaders agree that if their relationship with the government is poor, the community and the development activities suffer enormously (Table 1.46). It often leads to delayed release of grants by the government due to which even the execution of various programmes is delayed.

The respondents pointed out that there are training programmes run by the government for the Pradhans, Up-Pradhans and the ward members from time to time at the block and district levels to provide training in the village administration, panchayat functions, judicious use of powers and financial administration. There are also other programmes organized by health and education departments in which they are provided awareness about various diseases and educational programmes respectively. But none of the leaders reported any training programme organized for them at the state level. They feel that such programmes benefit the leaders by informing them about various issues of social concern, development schemes, development programmes and so on. Besides the training organized by the government agencies, there should also be certain initiatives taken by the governmental and non-governmental organizations.

Conclusion

Thus, the findings of the study show that in Himachal Pradesh, the absence of an oppressive social order, rise in literacy, improvement in the economic conditions and employment opportunities offered by the state have provided Dalits confidence and capability. Reservations have brought them into the new panchayats giving them representation and other opportunities that they did not enjoy earlier. The panchayats have, hence, become more inclusive than in the past. This is true in the case of Dalit women as well who now enjoy a better position in the state than in many other regions due to the traditionally better status and access to literacy.

However, this does not mean that Dalits participate as equal members in the panchayats in Himachal Pradesh. They have still to overcome the low social status they have occupied historically. They still do not have full access to decision-making, which remains the preserve of the better off sections of the village. But, the process of including them has begun and they are making steady inroads into areas not open to them earlier. Many of them have begun to enjoy the benefits provided by the new panchayats. As we shall see in the next three chapters, their position is much better than in the other states lying in the Gangetic plains selected for study.

3

Dalit Leadership in Panchayats in Uttar Pradesh

A Case Study of Shivegarh (Rae Bareli)

Uttar Pradesh (UP) provides a contrast to Himachal Pradesh in many ways. Spread over 2,38,566 square kilometres in 70 districts, India's second largest state, it is one of the most backward states in the Indian Union. On all basic indicators of development, it lags behind almost all other states. Only 41.6 per cent of the population is literate, which is below the national average, its Human Development Index at 0.110 in 1991 is the country's lowest, the rate of per capita income has been consistently below the national average from 1960-61 onwards, nor has its industrial progress been significant despite having a fairly large and diversified base. In agriculture, there was considerable growth during the Green Revolution period but no attempt was made to develop agro-industry and agricultural growth has now reached a plateau. This backwardness or the 'inertia' that has characterized this state, is to a large extent because its society remains steeped in social and gender inequality (Dreze and Gazdar, 1997: 31). The upper caste/class elite retained until recently fairly control over society, economy and polity. Extreme inequalities of political power excluded large sections of the population from effective participation in the democratic process. As a result, both economic and social changes have been slow and in fact delayed. While these features are found in many other states also, in UP two characteristics – *pervasive inequality* and *resilient conservatism* – make change very difficult (ibid: 101).

In such a setting, as the most disadvantaged social group, Dalits have suffered from low social status and disabling poverty in this state. Despite provision of protective discrimination by the state, low levels of literacy, lack of employment and the continuation of untouchability have kept them depressed. UP has 29.3 million Dalits, who constitute 21.04 per cent of its population against 16.48 per cent in India. The vast majority of the Dalits live in the rural areas. In 1991 census, they made up 23.16 per cent of the rural and 12.51 per cent of the urban population. The percentage of urban Dalit population to the total population in the state is only 11.31 per cent. Dalits are therefore less urbanized than the rest of the population, for whom the respective figures are 76.67 per cent and 87.43 per cent, and have not benefited from the processes of modernization and urbanization since independence.

Until recently, Dalits remained politically passive forming a vote-bank of the Congress party, which dominated the state. However, since the early 1980s, UP has experienced a strong wave of Dalit assertion and based upon it political mobilization. The reasons for this lie in rapid democratization and increasing politicization among the Dalits, accompanied by economic development in the state. From the late 1970s, scholars have pointed out that the economy of UP has "awakened out of its slumber" (Papola, 1989: 65). Its general rate of economic growth in the 1980s was higher than the national average both in agriculture and industry, and backward regions such as eastern UP have experienced substantial improvement in agriculture. However, these changes have taken place in only a few parts of the state, and the question remains how far Dalits – given their backwardness –

have been able to take advantage of these changes. At the same time, socio-economic and political changes have thrown up a new Republican, educated, upwardly mobile and assertive generation among the Dalits, who have rejected the Congress party and supported the Bahujan Samaj Party (BSP) that is a product of these changes. Social churning has led to conflict and confrontation between the upper and lower castes, which also witnessed in caste atrocities in the state. While economic development has provided the underlying potential to challenge upper caste domination, it is the emergence of Dalit identity and political mobilization that has been the lever of change among Dalits.

The BSP, which had formed the government in coalition with the Samajwadi Party (SP) and the Bharatiya Janata Party (BJP) in the state, has provided Dalits self-confidence and brought them into the mainstream of politics. Dalits are no longer prepared to accept oppression and domination leading to conflict and a steep rise in caste-based atrocities in recent years. Unlike in Himachal Pradesh, political parties have in recent years played a central role in panchayat elections reflecting the antagonism and competition between the Dalits and the OBCs represented by the BSP and the SP respectively. In the recent panchayat elections, held in November 2005, the BSP has performed well. Against the backdrop of these changes, our study of Shivegarh panchayat explores the changes taking place at the local level in this important state.

Sample District and PRIs

Uttar Pradesh was the first state to pass the UP Panchayati Act in 1949. The Shivegarh block of Rae Bareli has the distinction of having a Dalit MLA in the first state assembly election held in 1952. He openly championed the cause of Dalits in his constituency and challenged the interests of the upper castes and was murdered in July 1964. This incidence created awareness among the Dalits in the region leading to their organization and mobilization. Rae Bareli district is part of the Lucknow division and is bounded by Mohanlal Ganj and Haidergarh tehsils of Barabanki district. The southern boundary is formed by the Ganga, which separates it from the district of Fatehpur. It has a total population of 28,72,335, of which about 15 per cent are Dalits. Literacy levels among the Dalits are at the level of the state.

In this study, 12 village panchayats were selected within Shivegarh block of Rae Bareli district. In these panchayats, a total of 164 respondents – 77 Dalits and 87 non-Dalits – were interviewed. The Dalit respondents consisted of 48 men and 29 women: 6 in each category being Pradhans and the rest members. Four sub-castes among the Dalit representatives of the area, namely, Chamar, Pasee, Dhobi and Koree, were included, keeping in mind their proportion in the general population: 56 were Pasees and 16 Chamars, the two largest sub-castes in the district while a smaller number were Dhobis and Korees. The non-Dalit respondents consisted of 55 men and 32 women: again 6 in each category being Pradhans rest being members. While 28 belonged to the upper castes and 55 from the BCs, the rest being Muslims. Thus, the field study covered all the 164 Dalit and non-Dalit leaders – men and women – in the 12 village panchayats three each headed by Dalit and general caste men and women. Focused discussion with 15 development functionaries were also carried out to understand the relationship between the new Dalit leaders and the local bureaucracy. The records of meetings of the village panchayat were also scrutinized.

It is interesting to note that Dalits have been elected to panchayats in the sample block even before the passage of the 73rd constitutional amendment. Out of 77 respondents, 18 claimed that a family member had been elected earlier. Only one family member of a respondent had been elected Pradhan in 1985, the rest being panchayat members, 67 respondents stood for election only after the passage of the amendment on a reserved seat. Most Dalit leaders were able to win only once or twice in some cases. The main reason according to respondents is either lack of support or knowledge about the tactics required to win election, and these aspects are discussed later in the chapter.

Profile of the Respondents

There are marked differences in the socio-economic profile of the Dalit and non-Dalit respondents, which, as our study will show, impact upon their functioning within the panchayats. Tables 2.1 to 2.6 provide the age, education attainments, landownership pattern and income of the Dalit and non-Dalit respondents. The 73rd constitutional amendment, by providing reservation to Dalits, has brought a young, dynamic generation into the panchayats. Among them, 25.97 per cent of the Dalit respondents are in the age group of 20-30 and 46.76 per cent in 30-40. Only a little over 15 per cent are over 50 years of age. However, while the new leadership is young, about 30 per cent are illiterate and about 36 per cent are just literate, i.e., more than 65 per cent have none or hardly any literary skills. Less than half the respondents have been to school and only about 4 per cent are graduates or post-graduates. A second disadvantage faced by Dalits in village society is high landlessness. Among them 16 per cent are landless and the rest,

Table 2.1

Age of Dalit and non-Dalit leaders: Shivegarh

Age (in years)	*Dalit*	*Percentage*	*Non-Dalit*	*Percentage*
20-30	20	25.97	15	17.24
30-40	36	46.76	37	42.53
40-50	19	24.67	21	24.13
50-60	7	9.00	8	9.20
60-70	3	3.90	6	6.90
70-80	2	2.60	-	-
Total	77	100.00	87	100.00

Table 2.2

Educational status of Dalit and non-Dalit leaders: Shivegarh

Educational status	*Dalit*	*Percentage*	*Non-Dalit*	*Percentage*
Illiterate	23	29.87	12	13.79
Just Literate	27	35.06	19	21.84
Primary	7	9.09	11	12.64
Middle	9	11.69	14	16.09
High School	6	7.79	8	9.29
Intermediate	2	2.60	14	16.09
Graduate	2	2.60	6	6.90
Post-Graduation	1	1.30	2	2.30
LLB	-	-	1	1.15
Total	77	100.00	87	100.00

Table 2.3a

Ownership of irrigated land by Dalit leaders: Shivegarh

Landownership (in biswas)	*Dalit*	*Percentage*
Landless	16	20.78
4	2	2.60
6	2	2.60
8	3	3.90
10	9	11.68
20	7	9.09
30	15	19.48
40	10	12.99
50	4	5.18
60	3	3.90
70	1	1.30
80	3	3.90
90	1	1.30
120	1	1.30
Total	77	100.00

Average 27.21

Table 2.3b

Ownership of irrigated land by non-Dalit Leaders

Landownership (in biswas)	*Non-Dalit*	*Percentage*
1-10	5	5.75
10-20	12	13.79
20-40	13	14.94
40-60	11	12.64
60-80	5	5.75
80-100	5	5.75
100-120	4	4.60
120-140	2	2.30
140-160	6	6.90
160-180	1	1.15
220-240	1	1.15
240-260	3	3.45
280-300	1	1.15
300-320	1	1.15
320-400	1	1.15
Landless	16	18.39
Total	87	100.00

Average 71.38

Note: 1 acre = 32 *biswas* or 1.6 *bighas*

Table 2.4

Agricultural implements and machines owned by Dalit leaders: Shivegarh

Ownership of equipments	*No. of respondents*	*Percentage*
Tractor	7	17.07
Tubewell	16	39.02
Pumpingset	22	53.66
Thrasher	5	12.20
Base	41	-

except for 25 who own between 30-40 bighas (1 acre=32 biswas or 1.6 bighas), own very small plots. Few Dalits possess agricultural implements and machines that could enhance production. Moreover, the survey showed that only 9 out of 77 respondents have been able to obtain extra land for sharecropping. Low literary skills and landlessness are two characteristics that place Dalits at a disadvantage vis-à-vis upper castes/classes in the panchayats.

Table 2.5

Main occupation of Dalit and non-Dalit leaders: Shivegarh

Occupation	*Dalit*	*Percentage*	*Non-Dalit*	*Percentage*
Agriculture	32	41.56	34	39.08
Shopkeeping	1	1.30	-	-
Washing cloths	1	1.30	-	
Wage labours	21	27.27	13	14.95
Household work	22	28.57	29	33.33
Service	-	-	3	3.45
Caste occupation	-	-	8	9.19
Total	77	100.00	87	100.00

Table 2.6a

Annual income of Dalit leaders: Shivegarh

Income (in Rs.)	*Dalit*	*Percentage*
No income	24	28.57
7000-10000	31	40.26
10000-15000	9	11.69
15000-20000	2	2.60
20000-25000	8	10.38
25000-30000	4	5.20
30000-35000	1	1.30
Total	77	100.00

Average = Rs. 13336.36

Table 2.6b

Annual income of the non-Dalit leaders: Shivegarh

Income (in Rs.)	*Non-Dalit*	*Percentage*
7000-12000	36	41.38
12000-17000	7	8.04
17000-22000	3	3.45
22000-27000	5	5.75
27000-32000	2	2.30
32000-37000	3	3.45
37000-42000	2	2.30
42000-50000	1	1.15
No income	28	32.18
Total	87	100.00

A majority of Dalit leaders are found to be engaged in agriculture. While 32 per cent are farmers owning small plots, 21 per cent are wage labourers, another 22 per cent work as household workers in the village and a small section, namely, Dhobis, washes clothes. Thus, there has been no diversification of occupation away from agriculture reflecting the low educational level of the respondents. Although, the total family income of Dalit leaders is not high, there is considerable variation with 20 families having an income of only 7-10 thousand annually and two families having 40 to 45 thousand.

In contrast, the non-Dalit leaders are somewhat older, as only 3.45 per cent falling in the age group of 20-30 years, 17.23 per cent in 40-45 years and 6.90 per cent in 60-65 years. They are better educated than the Dalit leaders. Among them, 13.79 per cent are illiterate, but more respondents have been to school as the percentage of intermediate, graduates and post-graduates are more. Similarly, although, there are no big landowners in these villages and 18.39 per cent are landless, non-Dalits own more land. Most of them are medium landowners holding between 10-60 biswas of land – the average being 73.31 biswas in contrast to 27.21 biswas for the Dalit respondents. More than half (53.66%) of the non-Dalits own a pumpset, whereas 39.02 per cent own a tubewell and 17.07 per cent a tractor, which enable them to use their land more profitably. And 39.08 per cent of the non-Dalits are still engaged in agriculture, though, only 14.95 per cent are wage earners, but there has been a slight diversification towards service by 3.45 per cent of the respondents. These characteristics have, however, not translated into much higher income except among a small elite minority. However, 32.18 per cent of the respondents claimed that they had no income, the average earning of a little over 14 thousand is not higher than that of the Dalit respondents but the number of those in the higher income brackets is higher. While there are no Dalit respondents with an annual income of over 35 thousand, among the non-Dalits, a small section earns between 32 and 50 thousand. Thus, a small minority that belongs to the upper castes is better educated, owns more land and earns a higher income and is thus able to dominate in the village. Our study examines whether this minority is still dominant in the sample villages or due to reservation and assertion Dalits have been able to gain some control and participate meaningfully in the new panchayats.

As most Dalits have not stood for elections earlier, respondents were questioned about the factors that led them to contest elections to the new panchayats. Table 2.7 shows that a majority of the respondents held that they were persuaded by somebody to contest. Family members and supporters of respondents were instrumental in persuading the person to face the election. Former Pradhans and former members of the panchayat also played an important role in pushing respondents to stand for election. Table 2.8 suggests that the major motivating factors, which led respondents to stand for election, included village development, promotion of public interest and service to the poor. Only nine members could not identify any reason. Thus, there was enthusiasm among the Dalit members to join the panchayat and participate in the development of the village.

Table 2.7

Incidence of contesting election on own or on persuasion by somebody else: Shivegarh

	No. of respondents	*Percentage*
On their own	29	37.66
On persuasion by somebody else	48	62.34
Total	77	100.00
Persuaders		
Husband	14	29.17
Family members	21	43.75
Ex-Pradhan	9	18.75
Ex-members	12	25.00
Supports	37	77.08
Base	48	

Table 2.8

Motivating factors and forces behind contesting elections by Dalit leaders: Shivegarh

Motivating factors and forces	*Dalit*	*Percentage*
Allotment of land to landless	4	5.20
Village development	52	67.55
Eradication of factionalism and restoration of village unity	2	3.60
Promotion of public interest	38	46.75
Service to the poor	24	31.16
Deference to the wished and desires of family members and friends	6	7.79
Can't say	9	11.70
Base	77	

Table 2.9

Factors that helped in the success of Dalit leaders in elections: Shivegarh

Facilitating factors and forces in success	*Dalit*	*Percentage*
Religion	77	100
Caste-based reservation	77	100
Money	77	100
Cooperation of bureaucrats	24	31.66
Support of political parties	12	15.58
Blessings of Purohits (family priests)	59	76.62
Support of influential ex-zamindars	17	22.07
Support of influential persons of upper castes	44	58.44
Support of former leaders of village panchayat	51	66.23
Base	77	

Table 2.10

Difficulties faced while contesting elections: Shivegarh

Difficulties faced	*No. of respondents*	*Percentage*
Lack of money	69	89.61
Threats from rivals	47	61.04
Base	77	

Table 2.9 gives the factors that facilitated the victory of Dalit leaders in the election. Reservation based on caste provided by the constitutional amendment and money emerge as the most important reasons together with the support of influential persons in the village such as landowners, former leaders, members of upper castes or the priest. It is important to note that the support of political parties emerges as the least important factor that could help a Dalit candidate to win an election. A number of significant conclusions can be drawn from the data. All Dalits seem to agree that without reservation the chances of their winning the election were poor. This indicates that caste-based hierarchy and conservative social structure still retain importance. Moreover, the village is not a democratic public space in which merit, capability and honesty of candidates are determining factors, nor the traditional power

structure based on religion, land and caste has not broken down. This is supported by Table 2.10, which shows that most respondents agreed that the major difficulties faced were either money or threats from rivals.

Functioning of Dalit Leaders in the Panchayat

Awareness of panchayat programmes is necessary for the effective participation of Dalit leaders. Under the new panchayat system, leaders of the village panchayats have to initiate a wide variety of works to promote development particularly through schemes launched from time to time. Table 2.11 reveals that 71.26 per cent of the Dalit leaders are aware of the existence of various schemes such as the IRDP, TRYSEM, Jawahar Rozgar and Indira Awas Yojna that are aimed at helping the weaker sections. But more respondents know about older schemes such as the Jawahar Rozgar Yojna and TRYSEM that are no longer functioning in these districts than the new ones such as the Swarna Jayanti Gram Swarojgar Yojna and the Gram Sarak Yojna, which are operative at present. This points to a gap in their knowledge and affects the benefits that flow from these schemes to the Dalit community.

Table 2.11

Knowledge of village development schemes among the non-Dalit leaders: Shivegarh

Knowledge	*No. of respondents*	*Percentage*
Yes	62	71.26
No	25	28.74
Total	87	100
Actual schemes		
Jawahar Rozgar Yojna	77	100
Indira Avas Yojna	67	87.01
Swarna Jayanti Gram Swarojgar Yojna	29	37.66
Pradhan Mantri Gram Sarak Yojana	62	80.31
TRYSEM	77	100
Base	77	

Table 2.12

Methods adopted and reasons for success of village development schemes implemented by Dalit leaders: Shivegarh

Methods	*No. of respondents*	*Percentage*
Getting the necessary resolution passed in the meeting of Village Panchayats	69	87.34
Getting the approval of concerned ward member	34	43.04
Contacting the Pradhan and requesting and influencing him/her	51	64.56
Base	79	
Reasons for success		
Cooperation of villagers	69	89.61
Cooperation of Pradhan	32	41.56
Cooperation of BDO and other functionaries of block	27	35.06
Cooperation of members of Village Panchayats	72	93.51
Base	77	

Table 2.13

Acquaintance, relationship and assistance received by Dalit leaders from Block Pramukh and BDC members: Shivegarh

Acquaintance	*No. of respondents*	*Percentage*
Yes	29	37.66
No	48	62.34
Total	77	100.00
Nature of relationship		
Cordial	11	37.93
Strained	-	-
Neither cordial nor strained	18	62.07
Total	29	100.00
Assistance received		
Yes	22	75.86
No	7	24.14
Total	29	100.00

Table 2.14

Acquaintance, relationship and assistance received by Dalit leaders from Adhyaksha and members of Zila Panchayat: Shivegarh

Acquaintance with Adhyaksha and Members of Zila Panchayat	*No. of respondents*	*Percentage*
Yes	24	31.17
No	53	68.83
Total	74	100.00
Nature of relationship		
Cordial	5	17.24
Strained	-	-
Neither cordial nor strained	24	82.76
Total	29	100.00
Availability		
Yes	3	10.34
No	26	89.66
Total	29	100.00

Table 2.15

Opinion of the non-Dalit leaders regarding factors responsible for success in implementing development schemes: Shivegarh

Factors for success	*Non-Dalit*	*Percentage*
Cooperation of member of Gram Sabha	47	75.81
Cooperation of Pradhan	45	72.58
Cooperation of member of Gram Panchayat	37	59.68
Cooperation of BDO and the functionaries of block	32	51.61
No response	13	20.97
Base	62	

As is shown in Table 2.12 that majority of Dalit leaders (87.34%) point out that they are able to get schemes for the weaker sections implemented by getting the required resolutions passed in the meeting, and obtaining the approval of ward members as well as the Pradhan. This is possible largely due to the support of the members of the village panchayat (83.51%) and the villagers (89.61%) and to a lesser extent the Pradhan (41.56%). Only 35.06 per cent of the respondents held that they were able to gain the cooperation of the BDO and other officials of the block. Thus, problems of implementation of programmes by Dalit leaders are as much due to the conservatism of village society as the local bureaucracy. This is evident from Table 2.13, where 62.34 per cent of the respondents point out that they are not acquainted with the BDO and Block Pramukh and 62.07 per cent held that their relationship with these two functionaries is neither "cordial nor strained". But 75.86 per cent agreed that they were able to gain the requisite help from these functionaries when required. A similar picture emerges from Table 2.14 regarding the relationship with officials at the Zila Parishad with the vital difference that little help seems to be forthcoming from them to the village panchayat when required. Thus, while the local bureaucracy is responsive to the assistance requested by Dalit leaders – even though close relationships do not exist – this is not true at the district level. As much as 68.83 per cent of the respondents were not acquainted with, and 89.66 per cent felt that support to the Dalit leadership was not forthcoming from the district level. This could be a major handicap to a new struggling Dalit leadership at the grassroots level. As Table 2.15 points out, the experience of the non-Dalit leaders is similar. More respondents pointed to the cooperation received from the Gram Sabha, the Gram Panchayat and the Pradhan than from the BDO and other functionaries.

All the Pradhans have constituted the committees related to different aspects of development in the village. These committees are convened often depending on the kind of programmes running in the village. The Gram Sabha meetings are convened at least once a year but are held more often depending on need. Attempts are made to inform all the villagers so that they can attend the meetings. All government functionaries, such as the BDO, Village Level Workers (VLW) and development officers of all departments, attend the meetings.

For effective functioning of the panchayat, those elected must be able to mobilize resources, make decisions and ensure implementation of programmes with the help of the local functionaries and cooperation of the local population. Dalit leaders judged their performance in getting various developmental tasks for the village as equal to that of their predecessors (Table 2.16). The major programmes that they had been able to successfully implement were among others village development, flush latrines and laying of bricks. However, as Table 2.17 indicates, they faced a number of problems in doing so. The major obstacle was not caste-based discrimination as much as illiteracy and lack of social awareness and non-cooperation from villagers and even leaders who opposed change particularly the attempt by women to work in the panchayat for village development. The second problem was envy and jealousy, character assassination, withdrawal of facilities by powerful groups, non-cooperation from various factions and powerful sections who tried to protect their vested interests, false complaints etc. However, at least 23.38 per cent respondents pointed to non-cooperation from development functionaries and 15.58 per cent to delay in the release of funds sanctioned for development works. Thus, the new Dalit leadership is facing two types of challenges at the grassroots level: the traditional power holders who have long enjoyed dominance in village and panchayat affairs and a bureaucracy, which is not supportive to the needs of the Dalit leadership.

Table 2.16

Opinion of Dalit leaders regarding quality and type of work executed by them compared to their predecessors in the village panchayats: Shivegarh

Opinion	*Dalit*	*Percentage*
Better than that of their predecessors	19	24.68
Worse than that of their predecessors	-	-
Like that of their predecessors	58	75.32
Total	77	100.00
Type of work executed		
Getting the bricks laid on village lanes	8	42.11
Getting the drains constructed	3	15.79
Getting the earthen roads constructed	4	21.05
Getting the pour flush latrines constructed	9	47.38
Getting the houses constructed under the Indira Avas Yojana	7	36.84
Getting the village development work done	19	100.00
Base	19	

Table 2.17

Problem and difficulties faced by Dalit leaders in executing developmental programmes: Shivegarh

Problems and difficulties	*No. of Respondents*	*Percentage*
Non-cooperation from various factions	45	58.44
Deliberate and planned efforts by rivals made to find faults in work	24	31.17
Unnecessary envy and jealousy	36	46.75
Opposition for the sake of opposition	18	23.38
Efforts made by powerful sections to protect their vested interests and organised opposition in case of any threat to them	9	11.69
False complaints	6	7.79
Personal vilification and character assassination	17	22.08

Contd...

Contd...

Implication in false cases	2	2.6
Withdrawal of facilities by powerful sections	8	10.39
Non-cooperation from development functionaries	18	23.38
Delay in release of funds sanctioned for development schemes	15	15.58
Traditional social system not permitting women to go out of the four walls of their houses and to work in public	15	19.48
Male dominated social system in which males as husbands, father and brothers want to retain authority in their hands and to use women as their stooges	6	7.79
Illiteracy among leaders in particular, and members of Gaob Sabha in general	54	70.13
Lack of social awareness among leaders in particular and members of Gram Sabha in general;	27	35.06
Inter caste and sub caste distance	9	11.69
Inter-community distance	3	3.9
Base	77	

Table 2.18

Measures suggested by Dalit leaders for tackling the problem faced by them: Shivegarh

Measures suggested	*No. of Respondents*	*Percentage*
Education and training	54	70.13
Organization of inter-caste and inter community	39	50.65
Promotion of women's participation in economically gainful works	36	46.75
Base	77	

Faced with these obstacles, a majority of the Dalit leaders (70.13%) felt that education and training were required to overcome them (Table 2.18). But, at the same time, half of them (50.65%) were of the opinion that measures to improve inter-caste and inter-community relationships were necessary to tackle the problems faced by the new Dalit leadership.

Among them, 46.75 per cent of the respondents pointed out that it was necessary to promote participation of women, if they were to play a meaningful role in the new panchayats. Thus, the problems faced by Dalits are embedded in the structure of village society, which remains hierarchical and patriarchal, and in the bureaucratic structure at the local level. An enlightened bureaucracy, however, could have helped in overcoming some of the obstacles faced which does not seem to be happening.

Many of the government functionaries, right from BDO to the VLWs, with whom discussions were held, pointed out that Dalit leaders, particularly women, are unable to function properly due to widespread illiteracy, lack of competence and ignorance of how the tasks are to be performed. They also lack confidence due to their weak financial position, deprivation of land and modern farm equipment, non-availability of suitable employment, etc. Most important is their low social status as till lately, they were oppressed and subjugated by the upper castes in the village. However, an effort is being made in this direction and many of them are learning to cope with their new responsibilities.

Social Relationship between Dalits and non-Dalits

For the effective functioning of the new panchayats, an important condition is the removal of caste-based discrimination without which the Dalit leaders will not be able to make use of the empowerment that reservation has attempted to provide them. An attempt was made through the interviews to understand the relationship between the Dalit and the non-Dalit leaders and how this reflected on the functioning of the panchayats. Non-Dalit respondents were reluctant to admit that the relationship between the two groups is not cordial at all times but acknowledged that there is no open hostility or conflict and violence. Table 2.19 shows that Dalit respondents were divided on whether they enjoyed a good relationship and were reluctant to describe their relationship as 'bad': 27.27 per cent held that this relationship was good, 50.65 per cent felt that it was neither cordial nor strained, but 22.08 per cent were prepared to state that their mutual relationships were strained. A similar situation was noticed in the relationship between the Dalit leadership and the upper castes with both sides not wanting to comment.

Table 2.19

Nature of relationship of Dalit leaders with non-Dalit leaders in village panchayats: Shivegarh

Nature of relationship	*No. of respondents*	*Percentage*
Cordial	21	27.27
Neither cordial nor strained	39	50.65
Strained	17	22.08
Total	77	100.00

Table 2.20

Nature of relationship of Dalit leaders with OBC leaders in village panchayats: Shivegarh

Nature of relationship	*No. of respondents*	*Percentage*
Cordial	6	7.79
Strained	23	29.87
Neither cordial nor strained	48	62.34
Total	77	100.00

Table 2.21

Opinion of the non-Dalit leaders regarding special efforts required to be made for the upliftment of Dalit: Shivegarh

Type of efforts	*No. of respondents*	*Percentage*
Education	59	67.82
Awareness generation	68	78.16
Employment	37	42.53
Creation of self-confidence	24	27.59
Base	87	

Table 2.22

Types of special effort made for fulfilment of interests of Dalits: Shivegarh

Types of efforts made	*No. of Respondents*	*Percentage*
Getting BPL cards prepared	19	65.52
Providing help in the sanction and disbursement of scholarship to the Dalit student	16	55.17
Getting the bricks installed on lanes in Dalit hamlets and bustees	13	44.83
Assisting in the boring of tube well	13	44.83
Helping in the sanction of pension	19	65.52
Creating opportunities for self-employment	9	31.03
Making arrangement for books needed by school going children	13	44.83
Base	29	

Rather than the upper castes, it is with the OBCs that the relationship of Dalits is strained. Only 7.71 per cent of the Dalit leaders pointed to a cordial relationship while 29.87 per cent said their relationship was strained (Table 2.20). The OBCs are the major landowners in the village and are carrying on profitable agriculture. The Dalits are mainly agricultural labour and the former tend to "exploit and abuse the labour of Dalits" in the village. This socio-economic relationship spills over into the functioning of panchayats, creating tension and often conflict. The relationship between the Dalit leadership and the Muslim community in the village is much better. Most non-Dalit leaders felt that some special efforts were required to help the Dalits improve their socio-economic situation. They pointed to the need to not only provide education but to generate awareness and self-confidence among the Dalits who are elected to the panchayats (Table 2.21). Some of the non-Dalits do make efforts to help the Dalits, as Table 2.22

shows, by getting them BPL cards, ensuring pension, helping in their children's education, getting lanes bricked in Dalit hamlets etc. But, only 33.33 per cent take the trouble, the large majority (66.67%) are not interested, which points to an indifferent relationship with the Dalits.

However, we find that no active discrimination seems to be practised. And 81.67 per cent of the non-Dalit respondents claimed that Dalits are accorded seating places in the panchayats equal to those of the non-Dalits (Table 2.23). When differences of opinion arise or Dalits take action in the interest of their community, over 70 per cent of the non-Dalit respondents held that they do not openly take offence or overtly react. However, 36.78 per cent admitted that they prohibit the Dalits from saying anything and 20.69 per cent admitted that they try to take revenge and harm them, but only 8.04 per cent openly rebuke them (Table 2.24). Thus, a change is taking place within the panchayats: while the Dalits are attempting to improve their control, the non-Dalits are reluctant to share power with them but do not use force or stop them as in the past. Both assertion by the Dalits, who are no longer prepared to put up with oppression as in the past and the granting of reservation that has brought them into the panchayats is responsible for this change. These factors seem to be more important than the improvement in education among the Dalits.

Table 2.23

Opinion of Dalit leaders on being allowed by non-Dalit leaders to sit at equal plane: Shivegarh

Opinion	*No. of respondents*	*Percentage*
Yes	71	81.61
No	16	18.39
Total	87	100.00

Table 2.24

Reaction of non-Dalit leaders against bold decisions made by Dalit leaders against the former's interests: Shivegarh

Reaction	*No. of Respondents*	*Percentage*
Prohibit them from saying any thing	32	36.78
Rebuke and shout at them left and right	7	8.04
Take internally but do not overtly react	61	70.11
Try to take revenge and harm them	18	20.69
Base	87	

Table 2.25

Ability of Dalit leaders to work within the panchayats: Shivegarh

Ability	*No. of respondents*	*Percentage*
Yes	32	36.78
No	27	31.03
Can't say/No response	28	33.18
Total	87	100.00

Table 2.26

Opinion of the non-Dalit leaders regarding problems encountered by Dalit leaders: Shivegarh

Problems	*No. of respondents*	*Percentage*
Varied kinds of obstructions created in the way of developmental work initiated by them	25	28.73
Irregularity and unpunctuality on the part of members of Village Panchayats in participating in its meetings	21	24.14
Lack of coordinator among members of Village Panchayats mainly because of illiteracy	17	19.54
Bribe taken by intermediaries	16	18.39
Lack of unity among Dalits themselves	28	32.18
No response	49	56.32
Base	87	

Questioned about the ability of Dalit leaders to perform work in the panchayats, non-Dalit respondents were again divided and reluctant to give a clear answer (Table 2.25). While 36.78 per cent agreed that Dalits are capable of performing work allotted to them, 31.03 per cent answered in the negative and as many as 33.18 per cent gave no response. A section of the non-Dalit leaders is critical of the manner in which Dalits function within the panchayat (Table 2.26). More than half (56.32%) gave no opinion on the working of Dalit leaders. But nearly one-fourth (24.14%) of the respondents argued that Dalits are irregular and unpunctual in attending panchayat meetings, 28.73 per cent held that they created all kinds of obstructions in the developmental work of the panchayats, 18.39 per cent held they took bribes from intermediaries, while 19.54 per cent pointed to lack of coordination among members of the village panchayat due to illiteracy. Consequently, Dalit leaders enjoy a poor image among the non-Dalit members of the panchayats.

Table 2.27 shows that a majority of the non-Dalit respondents feel that the major problems encountered by Dalit leaders in working within the panchayats lie within the Dalit community. They point out that Dalit leaders are divided along sub-caste lines (65.52%); lack the ability to protect and promote Dalit interests (48.28%); are incapable of organized and concerted action (43.68%); are selfish and prepared to sacrifice the interests of their community to promote their own (39.08%); or are protégés of those who helped them get elected and do not have any independent position (60.92%). In the light of these criticisms, some non-Dalit leaders suggested measures to enable Dalits to function better in the panchayats, though 52.87 per cent were reluctant and gave no response (Table 2.28). Some of the suggestions were prescription of educational qualification as part of the conditions of eligibility for contesting elections, regular presence of Dalit women leaders in the meetings, eradication of intermediaries between village leaders and block officers, husbands of women not allowed to

Table 2.27

Opinion of the non-Dalit leaders about ability of Dalit leaders to promote the interests of their community in the village panchayats: Shivegarh

Opinion	*No. of respondents*	*Percentage*
Dalit leaders lack inability to protect and prompted Dalit interest	42	48.28
Dalit leaders are themselves divided on the basis of sub-castes and lack in unity	57	65.52
Dalit leaders cannot do any organized and concerted action	38	43.68
Dalit leaders are proteges of those who have motivated them to contest and supported them to get them elected and do not have any independent identity	53	60.92
Dalit leaders are highly selfish and always have their own axe to grind and do not hesitate in sacrificing the Dalit interests for the sake of their own interests	34	39.08
Base	87	

Table 2.28

Measures suggested by non-Dalit leaders to enable Dalit leaders to function effectively: Shivegarh

Measures suggested	*No. of respondents*	*Percentage*
United action	41	47.13
Education and training of members and Pradhans of Village Panchayats	41	47.13
Regular presence of women members of village panchayats in their meetings	28	32.18
Prescription of educational qualifications as part of the conditions of eligibility for contesting election for membership of and for the post of Pradhans in Village Panchayats	9	10.34
Eradication of intermediaries who negotiate with leaders in Village Panchayat and functionaries of the Block Development Office	35	40.23
Husbands of women members of Village Panchayats not to be allowed to sit in the meetings to represent their spouses	26	29.88
No response	46	52.87
Base	87	

represent their wives at panchayat meetings, and the like. Dalit leaders on their part were reluctant to answer the question about their relationship with the non-Dalits. Little more than half (50.65%) the Dalit respondents held that their relationship with non-Dalit members within the panchayats were neither cordial nor strained (Table 2.29). Although, 27.27 per cent of the respondents held that their relationship was cordial, and at least 22.08 per cent felt it was strained.

Table 2.29

Nature of relationship of Dalit leaders with non-Dalit leaders in village panchayats: Shivegarh

Nature of relationship	*No. of respondents*	*Percentage*
Cordial	21	27.27
Neither cordial nor strained	39	50.65
Strained	17	22.08
Total	77	100.00

Table 2.30

Existence and forms of untouchability in the Gram Sabha as perceived by Dalit leaders: Shivegarh

Existence	*No. of respondents*	*Percentage*
Yes	49	63.64
No	28	36.36
Total	77	100
Form of untouchability		
Non-Dalits do not eat food sitting together in the village publicly though they do so in hotels and restaurants	47	95.92
Non-Dalits do not eat food in or drink water from utensils used by Dalits	49	100
Non-Dalits do not offer cot to Dalits to sit at equal plane	36	73.47
Non-Dalits do not give respect to Dalits when they visit them at their (non-Dalits) residence	49	100
Children of non-Dalits call even senior members of Dalit community by taking their first and without adding any words of respect	11	22.45
Base	49	

It is important to note that 63.64 per cent of the Dalit respondents stated that untouchability is still practised (Table 2.30), ranging from not eating together, not offering an equal sitting place in the panchayat or giving respect to Dalits when they visit non-Dalit homes. When Dalits visit non-Dalit homes, they are not allowed to sit on the cot but are offered a mat or seat made of paddy stalks (locally called 'Bidra') compelling them to sit on the ground. All the Dalits try to offer food and drink whenever any non-Dalit happens to visit their home for any work, but it is avoided on some pretext such as not being hungry. In fact, Dalit leaders mentioned that even the children of the non-Dalits did not accord even elderly Dalits respect and address them by name.

Dalits agreed that the functionaries of the panchayat do not ill-treat them or practise any kind of discrimination. This is not possible as Dalits lodge complaints against them with their superiors or even with political leaders. But, the upper caste/class members of the village often provide the official functionaries a number of facilities and hence they are provided preferential treatment in all programmes while the interests of Dalits are ignored. All the Dalit leaders have pointed to a very limited cooperation from government functionaries. In case of time-bound target-oriented Dalit themes also, they release the funds only when their palms are greased. Most ridiculous part is that these very officers who take money try their best to get the Dalit leaders held accountable for misappropriation or embezzlement, if any complaint is made and an enquiry is instituted.

Majority of Dalit leaders (74.04%) have also pointed out that in case of atrocities against Dalits, police generally adopt delaying tactics and take action only when their palms are greased or when some pressure from some influential person is exerted on them. And 15.58 per cent pointed out that the police give no attention to complaints relating to atrocities against Dalits (Table 2.31). In fact, 66.26 per cent of the Dalit leaders pointed out that even Dalit police officers do not take any action to help them while 20.74 per cent of them, expressed the view that Dalit police officers do not give any attention to them.

Thus, the atmosphere in which the panchayat has to function does not promote equality of participation between Dalits and non-Dalits. A majority of non-Dalit leaders (78.16%), as we have seen earlier, averred that there was need to take special measures to remove untouchability and for upliftment of Dalits (Table 2.31). Yet, at the same time, 66.67 per cent of non-Dalit leaders admitted that they have not made any effort towards fulfilment of interests of the Dalits (Table 2.32). There is little sincere effort being made to remove untouchability by the non-Dalits of the area, it suits them to keep the Dalits downtrodden, as they are able to exploit their cheap labour in the village and marginalize them in decision-making in the panchayats. Thus, it is not merely caste discrimination but economic and political reasons that allow untouchability and discrimination to continue.

Table 2.31

Opinion of Dalit leaders about response of police and Dalit police officers in case of atrocities against Dalits: Shivegarh

Type of response by police	*No. of respondents*	*Percentage*
No attention is given	12	15.58
Delaying tactics are adopted	57	74.04
Appropriate action is taken	8	10.38
Total	77	100.00
Type of response by Dalit officers		
Not giving any attention	16	20.74
Not doing any thing to provide relief	51	66.26
Taking appropriate action	10	13
Total	77	100.00

Table 2.32

Incidence of the making special efforts for fulfilment of interest of Dalits: Shivegarh

Incidence	*No. of respondents*	*Percentage*
Yes	29	33.33
No	58	66.67
Total	87	100

Table 2.33

Reasons behind not opposing averments made by non-Dalit against Dalit interests in the panchayats: Shivegarh

Reasons	*No. of respondents*	*Percentage*
Fear of public insult	23	85.18
Loss of money	18	66.66
Fear of assault	4	14.81
Fear of withdrawal of facilities	11	40.74
Fear of false implication in cases	7	25.92
Base	27	

As Table 2.33 indicates, the large majority are afraid of public insults by the non-Dalits, which most of them would not be able to fight against. Equally important, the rest are afraid of loss of money, assault, withdrawal of facilities and fear of implication in police cases. Thus, we find that non-Dalits are still able to control and dominate over the Dalits in many ways that would definitely impair their independent functioning in the panchayats.

Conclusion

Uttar Pradesh provides an example of a state where Dalits are attempting to improve their position in the new panchayats. Although, much political mobilization has taken place in the state, it has not impacted as yet upon the working of panchayats. A major problem is the high illiteracy and lack of knowledge about the functioning of the panchayats among the large majority of Dalits. While Dalit members attend all the meetings, they are not able to participate meaningfully and effectively in the deliberations of the institution. The non-Dalits are able to take action, which protects and helps their own interests and the Dalits are unable to resist such moves. Most Dalits agreed that they could only react mildly as they fear further insult, loss of money and fear of withdrawal of facilities etc. On the other hand, the non-Dalit leaders held that the Dalits were unable to perform according to expectations. Factionalism and lack of unity among Dalit groups is also another factor pointed out. The relationship between the two groups has been neither good nor bad but indifferent, which is not conducive to the functioning of the panchayats. The continuation of various forms of social discrimination, such as not eating together or offering a seat, has made it even more difficult for Dalits to make inroads into the power structure of the panchayats. However, there is evidence of some efforts by non-Dalit leaders to help the Dalits improve their position in the panchayats. But, there is little evidence of the local bureaucracy helping the new Dalit members in the functioning of the panchayats. In short, Uttar Pradesh presents an example of a state, which is in transition from the older panchayats, which were under the control of the higher castes to a more democratic system in which Dalits are accorded a position of equality in participation and decision-making.

4

Dalit Leadership in Panchayats in Madhya Pradesh

A Case Study of Sehore and Satna

Madhya Pradesh (MP) lies in the central region of India. Like UP, it is one of the larger states of the Indian Union. While together with UP, it shares the status of being one of the *BIMARU* states of North India, though some differentiation has emerged during the 1990s. During the period of Congress rule under Digvijay Singh, MP advanced in many fields, particularly literacy, which has also helped the Dalits. While Dalits constitute 15 per cent of the population of MP (Census 2001), most of them are located in the northern region of the state bordering eastern UP and Bundelkhand. However, in contrast to UP, Dalit assertion and awareness is lower in the state due to the lack of an upsurge from 'below', the continued presence of the Congress as a party of the lower castes, absence of a strong party led by Dalits such as the BSP and mobilization by a local leadership. While the BSP has a presence, it is a 'third force' limited to certain districts and has not been as successful as in UP. A second difference is the attempt made by the Congress Digvijay Singh government through its scheme of Gram Swaraj, introduced on January 26, 2001, to further involve disadvantaged groups in the new panchayats established after the 73rd Constitutional Amendment. It was part of the efforts since the mid-1990s by the MP government to decentralize responsibilities downwards. The goal was to break the control of the locally dominant landowning castes over the panchayat and empower the village community as a whole, giving the lower castes a chance to play a role in decision-making. It has been variously described as an attempt to move from representative to 'direct democracy' at the grassroots and as a bold experiment in local self-government which if successful would introduce a new era of local governance. The Digvijay government introduced two more schemes: distribution of Charnoi lands and the Education Guarantee Scheme aimed to help the weaker sections. It is against this backdrop of policies for weaker sections and their impact on the Dalit community that this study is focused.

The northern districts of MP that lie contiguous to UP – where the study area is located – have a high proportion of SCs forming up to 25 per cent of the population in about 10 districts. Hence, two districts, namely, Sehore and Satna, were selected for study. The Chamars, who form 7 per cent of the Dalits, are called Jatavs here and bear similarity to their brethren in UP. The Balais, Mehras, Gandas and Kolis make up around 1 per cent. Besides, there are also numerous smaller groups. Although, assertion is not as high as in UP, the influence of the BSP has been felt here. It is a backward region within the state and social problems such as child marriage, *purdha* system and untouchability are still rampant. The school dropout rate among girls is high. There are many Hindu temples in the region constructed by the upper castes into which Dalits are not allowed. The latter, in order to avoid conflict, do not try to enter into them.

Sample Districts: Sehore and Satna

Two districts from the northern region of the state, where Dalits constitute a high proportion of the population, namely,

Sehore and Satna, were selected for the present study. Located on the Bhopal-Indore National Highway, 39 kms from Bhopal, Sehore district is surrounded by Bhopal in the north, Raisen in the east, Hosangabad in the south-east, Sajapur in the north-west and Dewas in the west. The district has seven towns, five development blocks, 450 Gram Panchayats and five Janpad Panchayats. As per 2001 census, the population of the district is 10,78,912 with a sex ratio of 908/1000. About 20.4 per cent of the population consists of SCs and the area also has a considerable Muslim population too. Chamar, Dhobi and Nai are the major sub-castes among the SCs. There are a number of big landowners in the two main backward castes of Mewara and Kahati. Rajput, Brahmin, Kayastha and Baniya represent the upper castes in this region. The literacy rate in Sehore district is 63.83 per cent but is only 47.95 among women and 78.14 per cent among men. The literacy rate among the Dalits is lower.

Satna district lies on the Vindhyan plateau and its boundary marches with that of Banda district of UP. It is hence one of the northernmost districts of MP. It has total population of 18,70,104 and SCs constitute 16.4 per cent of the population that is higher than in many of the central and southern districts of the state. The literacy rate is almost the same as in Sehore. As in the case of Sehore, there are big landowners but much of the district is also forested restricting agricultural land.

Profile of the Respondents

Both Sehore and Satna are backward districts. Consequently, as the data show, there is little difference in the economic position of the large majority of Dalit and non-Dalit respondents. However, there is a very small elite minority among the non-Dalit respondents who are much better off. Second, as the data suggest, Dalits suffer from certain disadvantages that affect their ability to participate in the functioning of the panchayats despite being granted reservations.

Sehore district has five blocks and 450 panchayats. A total of 56 respondents, consisting of equal number of Dalits and non-Dalits from these panchayats, participated in the study (Table 3.1). However, 28 Dalits and non-Dalits each were interviewed, using a semi-structured schedule. They included 12 Sarpanch, 40 Panch and 4 Zila Parishad members each equally divided into both categories. Informal discussions with 12 Gram Sabha members and four government officials provided insights into the functioning of the PRIs. In Manjhagawan block of Satna district, there are 97 village panchayats, out of which 35 were selected for study. As Table 3.2 shows, the total number of respondents selected in Satna was 120, out of which 49 were Dalits (male and female) and 49 were non-Dalits (male and female) and the remaining 22 were panchayat officials.

Table 3.1

Status, caste and gender description of the respondents: Sehore

Respondents	*Dalit*		*Non-Dalit*		*Total*
	Male	*Female*	*Male*	*Female*	
Sarpanch	3	3	3	3	12
Panch	10	10	10	10	40
Gram Sabha members	3	3	3	3	12
ZP/JP members	1	1	1	1	4
Government officials	1	1	1	1	4
Case Study	1	1	1	1	4
Total	19	19	19	19	76

Table 3.2

Status, caste and gender description of the respondents: Satna

Caste	*Gender*	*Posts*				
		Sarpanch	*Up-sarpanch*	*Panch*	*Panchayat*	*Total*
Dalit	Male	0.5	-	26	01	32
	Female	03	-	15	-	18
Non-Dalit	Male	12	04	21	21	58
	Female	07	10	04	-	12
Total		27	05	66	22	120

Table 3.3
Profile of the respondents: Sehore

	Dalit		*Non-Dalit*	
	Frequency	*Per cent*	*Frequency*	*Per cent*
Age-group				
15-24	4	14	1	4
25-34	10	36	10	36
34-44	8	28	10	36
45-59	3	11	6	20
60+	3	11	1	4
Total	28	100	28	100
Landholding size				
Landless	10	36	2	7
Upto 2.5 acres	11	39	2	7
2.5 to 5 acres	4	14	8	29
5 to 10 acres	3	11	8	29
10 acres +	0	0	8	29
Total	28	100	28	100
Literacy and education				
Illiterate	9	33	9	33
Literate	7	25	7	25
Primary	5	18	5	18
Middle	4	12	4	12
Matric	2	8	2	8
U.G./P.G.	1	4	1	4
Total	28	100	28	100
Occupation				
Nothing	4	12	4	12
Labour	8	29	8	29
Agriculture	5	18	5	18
Labour+agriculture	8	29	8	29
Private job	2	8	2	8
Others	1	4	1	4
Total	28	100	28	100
Annual income				
Nothing	3	11	3	11
Upto 5000	3	11	3	11
5000-10000	17	60	17	60
10000-20000	2	7	2	7
20000+	3	11	3	11
Total	28	100	28	100

Table 3.3 provides the profile of the respondents of the selected Sehore panchayats in terms of their age, education, occupation and annual income. While there is not much difference in the age of Dalit and non-Dalit respondents, the former are better represented in the age group of 15-24 and correspondingly less in the age group of 45-59. The age of the Gram Sabha members in the sample is higher than that of the Sarpanchas and Panchas. Thus, reservation has thrown up some younger Dalit leaders in these panchayats, though they are not better educated than that of the older generation. The backwardness of the region is reflected in the fact that there is little difference in the educational attainment of majority of both the Dalit and non-Dalit respondents. Only 8 per cent and 4 per cent of the respondents respectively have passed matriculation and attained undergraduate or postgraduate degrees. But, the survey of the family members of the respondents showed that the number of illiterates is much higher among Dalits whereas the number of matriculates and college educated persons is much higher among the non-Dalits giving them an advantage.

Dalits have the further disadvantage of owning much less land than the non-Dalits. As Table 3.3 shows that 36 per cent of the Dalit respondents do not own land against 7 per cent of the non-Dalit respondents. Moreover, the plots owned by the former are much smaller being upto 2.5 acres, whereas most of the larger plots between 2.5 and 10 acres are concentrated in the hands of the latter and no Dalit owns land over 10 acres. Irrigation facilities are very poor in the sample villages. However, more non-Dalits have access to wells and tubewells than the Dalits: only five Dalit respondents have facility of well and tubewell for irrigation but 18 non-Dalits have this facility.

Large majority of the respondents, both Dalits and non-Dalits, reported agriculture and agricultural labour as their occupation. However, the number of Dalit respondents and their families working on land is much higher in these villages compared to the non-Dalits. None of the members of the Dalit community is engaged in government job or business while some families among the non-Dalits have members pursuing these occupations. The economic backwardness of the region is seen in the fact that 12 per cent of both the Dalit and non-Dalit respondents said that they have no occupation and 11 per cent said they have no income. However, 8 per cent of the Dalits and non-Dalits have private jobs, as they do not own land. The large majority of the respondents, both Dalits and non-Dalits, have an income between 5 and 10 thousand rupees. A small minority among 11 per cent of the non-Dalits earns over 20 thousand, which is lower than in the other states studied.

Among the leaders, 24 Dalit respondents are living in *Kachha* houses compared to 11 among the non-Dalits. A majority of the Dalit respondents fall below the poverty line. Indebtedness is found among both the Dalit and non-Dalit representatives but the savings rate is much higher among the non-Dalits with very few Dalit respondents able to save from their income. The survey found that 16 Dalits and 14 non-Dalits were under debt. However, while the former take loans from the local 'Sahukar' (moneylender) to meet unforeseen family expenditure like food, medical bills or marriages; the latter are able to get loans from banks and cooperative societies for productive purposes like agricultural development. The impact of this is seen in Table 3.4 which shows the agricultural and household assets owned by Dalit and non-Dalit respondents. More non-Dalits own ploughs, bullock carts and threshers than the Dalits and no Dalit owns a tractor, while 9 non-Dalits own tractors. In terms of household items, non-Dalits own twice the number of almost all items shown in the table.

Table 3.4

Agricultural/household assets: Sehore

Age group in years	*Dalit*						*Non-Dalit*					
	Frequency			*Percentage*			*Frequency*			*Percentage*		
	Yes	*No*	*To-tal*	*Yes*	*No*	*To-tal*	*Yes*	*No*	*To-tal*	*Yes*	*No*	*To-tal*
Agricultural Assets												
Plough	9	19	28	32	68	100	22	6	28	79	21	100
Bullockcart	5	23	28	18	82	100	15	13	28	54	46	100
Tractor	0	28	28	0	100	100	9	19	28	32	68	100
Thresher	1	27	28	4	96	100	14	14	28	50	50	100
Bullock	7	21	28	24	75	100	22	6	28	79	21	100
Harvester	0	28	28	0	100	100	0	28	28	0	100	100
Sprayer	2	26	28	7	93	100	15	13	28	54	46	100
Pumpset	4	24	28	14	86	100	20	8	28	71	29	100
Household Assets												
Cooler/fan	11	17	28	39	61	100	24	4	28	86	14	100
Bicycle	7	21	28	25	75	100	22	6	28	79	21	100
Two-wheeler	3	25	28	11	89	100	14	14	28	50	50	100
Four-wheeler	0	28	28	0	100	100	1	27	28	4	96	100
Radio/Tape	10	18	28	36	64	100	19	9	28	68	32	100
TV	6	22	28	21	79	100	21	7	28	75	25	100

Table 3.5

Reasons for not contesting next election: Sehore

Reasons	*Dalit*			*Non-Dalit*		
	Sar-panch	*Panch*	*JP Member*	*Sar-panch*	*Panch*	*JP Member*
No voice	-	2	-	-	-	-
Relatives will contest	-	2	-	-	-	-
Status degradation	3	1	-	-	-	-
Officials non-cooperative	-	-	1	-	-	-
No gain	2	-	-	-	-	-
Criticism	-	-	-	-	1	-
Personal loss	-	-	-	2	3	-
Total	5	5	1	2	8	1

Due to a variety of local and outside factors, the process of class and elite formation is going on among the Dalits as among other groups. With reserved posts Dalits have to compete with other Dalit members. In this situation the Dalit who is relatively more powerful is likely to be elected. In the study, it was found that a number of the members and sarpanchas were elected unopposed as they were perceived by the community to be more conscious and active. Thus, Dalits in the sample villages are hopeful that with reservation, they will benefit by having their own representative in the panchayat and expectations among the small minority who are aware and politically conscious is high.

But as Table 3.5 reveals, in both the Dalit and non-Dalit categories, an equal number (11) of respondents are not keen to contest elections again. Some of the reasons that have discouraged Dalits from contesting elections again is a feeling of voicelessness, ineffectiveness, status degradation and lack of cooperation from government officials. Among non-Dalit respondents, personal loss and particularly criticism were the major reasons for not contesting elections again. A number of representatives belonging to both the Dalit and non-Dalit categories are facing problems due to their panchayat duties and have decided not to stand for election again. While some gained benefits, many were unhappy with their experience. Among them 50 per cent Dalit and 46 per cent of non-Dalit respondents have decided not to contest the next panchayat election. They feel that since they cannot participate effectively in decision-making and extend benefits to villagers, therefore, it would be wrong on their part to represent them without doing anything for them.

The profile of the respondents in Satna district is similar to that of the Sehore district. Table 3.6 shows that there is not much difference in the age of the Dalit and non-Dalit respondents. A majority of the Dalit respondents are between the ages of 26 to 50 years, though 18.36 per cent fall into the age group of 51-55 years and one person is more than 60 years' old. In contrast, most of the non-Dalit leaders are in the age group of 26-40 years, 14.28 per cent are in 51-55 years and there is no person above 60 years of age. As Table 3.7 shows, about half (46.94%) of the Dalit respondents were illiterate and 22.44 per cent are just literate, only one has completed high school and one each had a graduate and post-graduate degree. Only three female Dalit respondents have attended primary school. The situation is better in Satna in the case of the non-Dalits than in Sehore as only 16.32 per cent were illiterate and 8.16 per cent just literate, a larger number have been to school and 11 respondents have completed intermediate and three have a graduate degree. While more Dalit female respondents have been to school, none of them have attended high school. Thus, the ability of non-Dalit respondents to participate in the panchayat due to better educational attainments is better than that of the Dalit respondents.

Table 3.6

Classification on the basis of age-group of Dalit and non-Dalit respondents: Satna

Age Group	*Dalit*						*Non-Dalit*					
	Male		*Female*		*Total*		*Male*		*Female*		*Total*	
	No.	*%*	*No.*	*%*	*No.*	*%*	*No.*	*%*	*No.*	*%*	*No.*	*%*
21-25	1	2.04	-	-	1	2.04	-	-	-	-	-	-
26-30	3	6.12	3	6.12	6	12.24	5	10.20	6	12.24	11	22.45
31-35	7	14.28	3	6.12	10	20.40	8	16.33	1	2.04	09	18.36
36-40	7	14.28	5	10.20	12	24.48	11	22.45	4	8.16	15	30.60
41-50	5	10.20	1	2.04	6	12.24	01	2.04	-	-	1	2.04
51-55	5	10.20	4	8.16	9	18.36	04	8.16	-	-	4	8.16
56-60	3	6.12	-	-	3	6.12	07	14.28	-	-	7	14.28
61-65	-	-	2	4.08	2	4.08	01	2.04	1	2.04	1	2.04
Total	31	63.27	18	36.72	49	100	37	75.51	12	24.48	49	100

Table 3.7

Education of Dalit and non-Dalit respondents: Satna

Education	*Dalit*						*Non-Dalit*					
	Male		*Female*		*Total*		*Male*		*Female*		*Total*	
	No.	*%*	*No.*	*%*	*No.*	*%*	*No.*	*%*	*No.*	*%*	*No.*	*%*
Illiterate	12	24.48	11	22.44	23	46.94	3	6.12	5	10.20	8	16.32
Primary	1	2.04	2	4.08	3	6.12	5	10.20	2	4.08	7	28.56
Junior High School	4	8.16	-	-	4	8.16	9	18.36	1	2.04	10	20.40
High School	5	10.20	-	-	5	10.20	5	10.20	-	-	5	10.20
Intermediate	1	2.04	-	-	1	2.04	11	22.45	-	-	11	22.45
Graduation	1	2.04	-	-	1	2.04	3	6.12	-	-	3	6.12
Post-Graduate	1	2.04	-	-	1	2.04	1	2.04	-	-	1	2.04
Literate	6	12.24	5	10.20	11	22.44	-	-	4	8.16	4	8.16
Total	31	63.24	18	26.72	49	100	37	75.51	12	24.48	49	100

Table 3.8

Occupation of Dalit and non-Dalit respondents: Satna

Occupation	*Dalit*		*Non-Dalit*	
	No.	*%*	*No.*	*%*
Only agriculture	12	24.48	26	53.06
Only labour	15	30.61	8	16.32
Service	2	4.08	-	-
Only rural business	6	12.24	-	-
Agriculture + rural business	3	6.12	2	4.08
Agriculture + pension	-	-	3	6.12
Agriculture + labour	11	22.44	6	12.24
Agriculture + service	-	-	4	8.16
Total	49	100	49	100.00

Table 3.8 shows that 24 per cent Dalit respondents depend on agriculture and a majority of them are labourers mostly in

agriculture, a few have set up rural businesses and two are in service. In contrast, 53.06 per cent, i.e., more than half of the non-Dalit respondents, depend on agriculture for their livelihood as they own much more land than the Dalit respondents. Only 16.32 per cent are labourers, while the rest combine agriculture with business and service. The non-Dalit respondents are economically much better off than the non-Dalits due to more land and better educational attainments. Thus, both our sample districts lying within a backward region are poor, but there is a small section among the non-Dalit respondents, which is much better off and has traditionally occupied an important role in the local panchayat. It is against this backdrop that the study attempted to understand the role played by the Dalit representatives and Sarpanchas in the sample panchayats.

In the sample panchayats almost half the Dalit respondents said that no Dalit had been elected before, while a few did not know when elections were held, or pointed out that elections were rarely held. As much as 44.90 per cent of the representatives in the sample were elected unopposed, most of them being Dalits. Most of the respondents, however, had been elected only for the first time (89.20%) and none for the third time. Thus, the large majority of the respondents are participating in the functioning of the panchayats for the first time. It is interesting to note that 57.14 per cent of the Dalit respondents stated that their main source of motivation was self-awareness, 22.45 per cent said it was their family while according to 20.40 per cent others motivated them. These are districts, where political consciousness is rising and this led many of the respondents to stand for panchayat elections. Among the leaders, 89.79 per cent of the Dalit respondents held that they had no political experience prior to being elected to the panchayat (Table 3.9) Table 3.10 shows that 20.40 per cent of the Dalit respondents where threatened by the non-Dalits in the village during the elections.

Table 3.9

Classification on the basis of political experience: Satna

Political experience	*Respondents*					
	Male		*Female*		*Total*	
	No.	*%*	*No.*	*%*	*No*	*%*
Yes	4	8.16	1	2.04	5	10.20
No	27	55.10	17	34.69	44	89.79
Total	31	63.26	18	36.73	49	100.00

Table 3.10

Rejection by non-Dalits in election, and forms of rejection: Satna

Political experience	*Respondents*					
	Male		*Female*		*Total*	
	No.	*%*	*No.*	*%*	*No*	*%*
Yes:						
(a) by threatening	7	14.28	3	6.12	10	20.40
(b) by physical torture	-	-	-	-	-	-
No	24	48.98	15	30.61	39	79.59
Total	31	63.27	18	36.73	49	100.00

Panchayat Functioning in Sehore

Awareness and knowledge about panchayat institutions, their structure and functioning is essential, if Dalits are to play a meaningful role and contribute to local development. The level of awareness of a group is directly related to use or adoption of development schemes. First, we deal with Sehore, where the survey revealed that about 75 per cent of the respondents did not know when the new PR system was established and had not even heard about the 73rd constitutional amendment. As Table 3.11 shows, 25 per cent of the Dalit and 21 per cent of the non-Dalit respondents were not aware of the objectives of the panchayats. Rest of the respondents held that PRIs were meant for village development, while some others felt that they were meant to provide work for villagers and provide social justice.

Table 3.11

Objective of new PRIs as perceived by the respondents: Sehore

S. No.	*Response*	*Dalit*		*Non-Dalit*	
		Frequency	*%*	*Frequency*	*%*
1.	No knowledge	7	25	6	21
2.	Total development	4	14	2	7
3.	Village development	7	25	6	21
4.	Construction in village	I	4	2	7
5.	Panchayat should take care of village	-	-	2	7
6.	Social justice/poor welfare	1	4	-	-
7.	Awareness	1	4		
8.	Villagers work in village itself	3	11	3	11
9.	Village problem to be solved in village	-	-	2	7
10.	Fulfil the dream of Gandhiji	-	-	1	4
11.	Political mileage	-	-	2	7
12.	Political purpose	-	-	1	4
13.	3+4	-	-	1	4
14.	2+3+4	2	7	-	-
15.	3+5	2	7	-	-
	Total	28	100	28	100

Likewise, there is little knowledge about the activities of panchayats, training for members and the rights and duties of the members. Table 3.12 unveils that 14 per cent of the Dalit respondents were not able to give any reply about the source of their information. The non-Dalit respondents were, on the whole, better informed. Most of the respondents (Dalit and non-Dalit) gained information from the panchayat meetings or from interaction with villagers and a lesser number from family members. Dalit respondents held that the block office was a better source of information than the Gram Sevak. There was also little knowledge about the electoral process or the date on

Table 3.12
Source of information: Sehore

S. No.	*Response*	*Dalit*		*Non-Dalit*	
		Frequency	*%*	*Frequency*	*%*
1.	No response	4	14	-	-
2.	Training	1	4	3	11
3.	Pnachayat meeting	8	29	7	25
4.	Interaction with villagers	5	18	4	14
5.	Not applicable	3	11	5	18
6.	Husband	1	4	1	4
7.	Gram Sevak	-	-	1	4
8.	Self thinking	2	7	2	7
9.	By reading act	-	-	2	7
10.	Family members	1	4	-	-
11.	Father	-	-	1	4
12.	Block office	1	4	1	4
13.	3+4	1	4	-	-
14.	4+8	1	4	-	-
15.	2+12	-	-	1	4
	Total	28	100	28	100

which the elections were held. The role of newspapers or the television seemed to be very insignificant. Most came to know about the elections from the earlier panchayat representatives. Similarly, only 4 per cent of the Dalit respondents and 11 per cent of the non-Dalit respondents knew about the training programmes conducted for them. With regard to increasing the level of information and awareness of the panchayat members, many suggested that frequent training programmes would be useful. However, the large majority argued that if panchayat discharge their duties properly and hold meetings and provide development in the village that itself could be a source of information and awareness. Discussion with the respondents also made it clear that about three-fourth, i.e., 20 out of the 28, Dalit respondents did not know that there is a specific percentage of reservation for them in the panchayat and that this facility is provided in all the eight committees formed under the Gram Sabha. Only one Dalit and five non-Dalit respondents were aware of the exact percentage of reservation for Dalits in the panchayats. Similarly, only six respondents knew how much of reservation has been granted to women in the panchayats.

In like manner, only a few respondents were found to be aware of their rights and duties as members of the panchayat. And, those who were aware were vocal about them. A total of Dalit and 11 non-Dalits respondents felt that the rights/powers granted under the Act are not sufficient to deal with village level problems and more should be given to them. Some argued that decisions taken in the Gram Sabha should be implemented without delay. As a woman Panch of Sikarpur panchayat held, "Grants released to the panchayat are disproportionately possessed by the Sarpanch. The amount should equally be divided for each of the wards. Today, the wards represented by the poor panch are neglected in this manner". Some of the respondents also argued that Panchas must also have the right to punish offenders. There is a strong feeling among the respondents that the interests of the poor are not looked after in the panchayats. Dalit respondents, despite their poor understanding of the manner in which panchayats function, were unhappy about this. As an SC respondent pointed out, "There are many laws but seldom are these implemented. It is the rich people who dominate in the panchayat. Because of the panchayat there is improvement in their social status. Nobody listens to the poor and the Dalit representatives. Hence, it is the government which can come forward and ask all the concerned to implement the existing laws and in case of noncompliance, they should be punished".

Some of the respondents were also unhappy with the manner in which the local bureaucracy functioned. For example, a non-Dalit Sarpanch of Thuna Kala panchayat stated,

"Power conferred on the panchayat is not sufficient in the real sense. The decision taken by the Gram Sabha and the proposals made out of these decisions are not always accepted by the administration. They should not alter/change it, otherwise the panchayat people feel humiliated".

Table 3.13

Educational background of the respondents who attended training programme: Sehore

Education	*Training Programme*	
	Dalit	*Non-Dalit*
Illiterate	1	-
Literate	2	2
Primary	1	1
Middle	1	1
Matric	-	1
Total	5	5

As Table 3.13 shows, only five Dalit and non-Dalit respondents each have attended training programmes. Due to their low educational level, they were not able to fully benefit from the programme. The training programme was for only a few days and respondents held that it was related to agriculture, environment, panchayat rules and functioning and village development. Among them eight Dalit and nine non-Dalit respondents felt that not only their knowledge about the panchayat increased due to the training programme, it also enhanced their self-confidence and they were able to share their experiences with the other members of the panchayat. Thus, the level of awareness and knowledge about the panchayat and its functions is quite low among the respondents but this is more marked in the case of Dalit respondents. The training programme is yet to reach out to larger number of panchayat representatives and is of too short duration to have a full impact. Nevertheless, it has played a significant role.

The Gram Sabha members were asked about the functioning of the Sarpanchas. More than half of them felt that the Dalit Sarpanchas are not performing well due to village politics, corruption, favouritism and manipulation. Consequently, they lose their integrity and are not respected by the villagers. One of the respondents pointed out, "The Sarpanch cannot do any of his work in the concrete sense of the term. The ex-Sarpanch was committed to do development work and he increased the income of the panchayat.... constructed shops and connecting roads, but the present Sarpanch is unable to do anything. He has no capacity". But, a Dalit member held that "neither the ex-Sarpanch nor the current Sarpanch is sensitive to the problems of the people. In my house, there is neither electricity nor drinking water facility. In spite of my meeting with the Sarpanch they (both the former and present) have failed to provide these facilities". Members agreed that the panchayat had been able to construct roads, school building, handpumps, houses and a latrine in the school. But they felt that other important works which would benefit the poorer sections such as land to the landless, houses for the poorer sections, PDS facilities, employment and health care facility have not been undertaken. Even the Dalit representatives, it was pointed out, once elected, they behave like 'monarchs' and have only helped a small section of the community, and the really poor sections have not been able to gain much. Moreover, it was felt that they have failed to deal with caste-based discrimination due to fear of non-confidence motion from the Gram Sabha.

Only a small section of the Dalit villagers attend the Gram Sabha meetings. It is organized about once a month but the required quorum is rarely fulfilled. Some respondents held that this is because people are not enthusiastic about attending meetings as they feel that they will not get anything. As one respondent pointed out, the meetings are held regularly but in at least 40-45 panchayats, out of the 127 in the region. The Sarpanchas motivate only their own supporters to attend the meeting, and they rarely invite others. But, most Dalits are unable to do so because they do not get information on time, are not properly invited, cannot leave their wage work or because they feel that they will not gain any benefits and there are quarrels in the meeting. However, many showed keenness in the functioning of the panchayat and have given suggestions which are often not heeded by the others. As Table 3.14 a shows, all the villagers have much expectation from the panchayat: BPL cards, better roads, drinking water, land, employment opportunities, health care etc. Some of the suggestions, they proffered, were: timely release of financial grant by the government, more training programmes for the panchayat representative and more development work by the panchayat.

Table 3.14a

Issues in terms of priority: Sehore

Respondents	
Dalit (Male)	Village development, construction of village road, school building, water facility, name inclusion in BPL list and pension facility.
Dalit (Female)	Facility of water, house, electricity, road and health.
Non-Dalit (Male)	Road, handpump, cleanliness and construction of common facility.
Non-Dalit (Female)	The proposal forwarded by the Gram Sabha/Gram Panchayat should be approved and implemented

Many of the villagers, irrespective of their caste background, were critical of the panchayat secretary and described him as uncooperative, corrupt, manipulative, and inattentive. Some felt that he had manipulated the old age pension. It was also felt that he was under the control of the Sarpanch and did not listen to the villagers or other members.

Both the Dalit and the non-Dalit respondents have to work with other representatives, local notables and government officials and maintaining cordial relation is essential. In course of the study, it was observed that non-Dalits were not keen to talk about their relationship with Dalits. While 15 non-Dalits said that they had good relationship with the Dalit representatives, the remaining held that the relationship was neither good nor bad. Similarly, three Dalits held that they had poor relationship with the non-Dalit representatives. One of the woman Dalit respondents observed that she found it difficult to work with them, as they had brought no-confidence motion against her. In the same way, at the Janpad Panchayat level, the nature of relationship between the Dalit and the non-Dalit members was described as neither good nor bad. In certain cases, panchayat secretaries are part of the government staff but in another case they are appointed by Sarpanch mainly on the basis of primordial considerations. Half of the respondents pointed out that their relations with panchayat secretary were good but 21 per cent Dalit and 11 per cent non-Dalit representatives complained that their relationship with the panchayat secretary was unsatisfactory. The secretary does not listen to them and in some of the cases has also cheated the panchayat representatives. The relations between government officials and political workers are by and large good but at the local level there are cases of tense relations, particularly with the local level influential people and the Dalit representatives.[*]

Majority of the Dalit representatives (71%) feel that reservation facility in itself is not sufficient for the empowerment of Dalit representatives in particular and Dalit masses in general. It opens door only for a limited number of people and that too to a limited extent. Only four Dalits perceive reservation facility as a sufficient condition for the development of Dalits as it provides opportunities to them to introduce a number of changes. One of the Dalit respondents felt that if the

* Narrated in the original study "Dalit and Tribal Leadership in Panchayats: A Case Study of Madhya Pradesh" PRIA: New Delhi, pp. 51-54.

government is really interested to empower Dalit masses, the upper limit of reservation should be increased. Among non-Dalit respondents 43 per cent said that it is a sufficient condition for the overall empowerment of the Dalit community. But, many Dalit representatives argued that reservation alone could not empower them in the absence of education, awareness, more legal rights, employment opportunities, etc. Moreover, they feel that if the existing change agents are corrupt, irresponsible or biased, then, the positive reference group for the Dalit elites who are still in making will be ineffective for the development of the Dalit masses. Therefore, it is essential that along with reservation facility other support systems should be made available to all the concerned at the community level.

Problems Faced by Dalits Members

Reservation is one of the preconditions to encourage and ensure participation of Dalits in panchayat activities. But it is not a sufficient condition because their actual participation depends upon a variety of personal and social conditions. In the past, Dalits were not members of the panchayats or very few succeeded in becoming members and were either passive observers or were coopted by the upper castes. But, due to the 73rd amendment, they have gained membership through direct elections. The study found that despite the provision of reservation, most of the Dalit respondents have many bitter experiences and face difficulties in discharging their duties because of the social environment. They pointed out that due to their low status in the village, nobody listened to their views and rejected their proposals, particularly in situations where the Sarpanch is a non-Dalit. A Dalit Panch of Lasuria panchayat said, "Since Dalits are less in number in the panchayat body, therefore, non-Dalit members do not listen to them. We often oppose their (upper castes) unacceptable views in the meeting unsuccessfully. People from the general category dominate in our panchayat. As Dalit representatives, we have failed to avail any benefit from the panchayat body". An important reason is the illiteracy of the Dalit respondents. A small Dalit farmer and Panch of Baragarh panchayat pointed out, "Sarpanch and others only send papers to me for signature. They never inform me so that I can attend a meeting".

However, at the same time, observation showed that Dalit representatives do not organize themselves, discuss and formulate strategies to overcome the problems created by the local and block level officials and non-Dalit representatives. Rather, they feel dependent upon and expect help from the administration, non-Dalit representatives and higher level panchayat functionaries.

Few panchayat representatives feel free to take independent decisions in the Gram Sabha or in panchayat committees on the basis of the merit of a particular case. However, Dalits are under greater pressure, as they are perceived as leaders of their community who can provide them help and benefits. Moreover, while both Dalit and non-Dalit respondents take help from others in their private life such as loans etc. The former, due to their poor economic situation, do so more often and hence are under greater pressure to fulfil the expectations of those who provided support to them during the election. Dalits also have to satisfy upper caste villagers due to whom they were elected. As much as 89 per cent of Dalit and 54 per cent of non-Dalit respondents pointed out that they are influenced in their decisions by others, both from within the panchayat body or outside (Table 3.14b). Among them, 25 per cent Dalit and 21 per cent non-Dalit asserted that they are unable to implement many collective decisions taken in Gram Sabha meetings by influential members because of lack of funds. Consequently, they loose their credibility and are criticized by Gram Sabha without understanding constraints. Here, 12 Dalit and 2 non-Dalit respondents stated that in many cases the Sarpanchas make their own decisions without consulting or taking the opinion of the Panchas. And one Dalit and two non-Dalit women representatives complained that their husbands decide everything and they just put their signature. And two representatives did not attend the meetings but willingly put signature as and when required, and again two respondents felt that in panchayat only the influential members make the decisions (Table 3.14b).

Table 3.14b

Reasons for not taking independent decision: Sehore

Response	*Dalit*		*Non-Dalit*	
	Frequency	*%*	*Frequency*	*%*
No response/No reply	-	-	2	7
Not applicable	3	11	12	43
Decision by Gram Sabha meeting	7	25	6	21
Sarpanch decides	12	43	2	7
Do not visit panchayat office	1	4	-	-
Everything done by husband	1	4	2	7
Signature without attending meeting	1	4	1	4
Decision by the influential	1	4	1	4
Nobody listens	-	-	2	7
JP members are heard	2	7	-	-
Total	28	100	28	100

Has reservation empowered the Dalits? Almost all the Dalit respondents replied in the negative together with half the non-Dalits. The former pointed out that most of the Dalit Sarpanchas are unable to do any substantial developmental work or help the community. In short, while some developmental work has happened, there is little empowerment or attention given to social issues for the Dalits.

Table 3.15

Problems of Dalit respondents: Sehore

S. No.	*Response*	*Dalit*		*Non-Dalit*	
		Frequency	*%*	*Frequency*	*%*
1.	No response	1	4	-	-
2.	Lack of school	1	4	2	7
3.	Lack of employment opportunity	4	14	3	11
4.	Check on physical movement	4	14	-	-
5.	Lack of drinking water/electricity/latrine	3	11	-	-
6.	Landlessness	2	7	2	7
7.	Lack of loan facility	1	4	-	-
8.	Inclusion in BPL list	1	4	-	-
9.	Difficulty in obtaining pension	-	-	2	7
10.	Alcoholism	-	-	1	4
11.	Lack of road/drainage	-	-	1	4
12.	No problem	1	4	4	14
13.	Do not get benefits from schemes	1	4	-	-
14.	2+3+5+13	2	7	3	11
15.	3+4+11+12	1	4	-	-
16.	3+5+9	I	4	1	4
17.	3+7+12	1	4	I	4
18.	3+7+10+11	1	4	-	-
19.	5+15	1	4	4	14
20.	6+7	1	4	2	7
21.	6+8	1	4	1	4
	Total	28	100	28	100

Table 3.15 shows that some significant works such as roads, bridges and drainage have been undertaken by respondents for the overall development of their respective panchayats and four non-Dalit respondents stated that Dalits do not face any specific problems. But many Dalits and non-Dalit representatives agree that some of the specific problems faced by the Dalits such as lack of employment opportunity, education facility, problem of migration, drinking water problem, landlessness, loan facility, inclusion of

name in BPL list etc., have not been addressed by either the Dalit nor the non-Dalit representatives. Equally important is untouchability, which is still practised in the study area and Dalits are discriminated against in many ways by the non-Dalit simply on the basis of caste. Among the Dalit respondents 79 per cent representatives held that untouchability is still practised in their villages but only eight non-Dalit respondents supported this view. The remaining non-Dalit respondents argued that it does not exist. However, all those who replied in the affirmative said that mainly social restriction is observed in the case of feeding and drinking. While 75 per cent Dalits feel that there is no effort on the part of panchayat to eliminate this problem, 29 per cent non-Dalits felt that untouchability is not practised and, therefore, the question of effort to deal with this problem does not arise. One of the Dalit respondents felt that since untouchability is a part of our tradition, therefore, there is no possibility to deal with this problem.

Some attempts such as inter-community dining and awareness generation programmes have been made by the panchayats to deal with this problem but these have been quite irregular. Besides untouchability, there are some other problems specifically found among Dalits. Among the respondents, 18 per cent Dalit and 21 per cent non-Dalit said that alcoholism is rampant among them and a significant number felt that if Dalits are prohibited from consuming liquor, anti-liquor programmes organized and employment opportunities provided by the government at the local level, this problem could be eradicated. Besides this, the problem of internal infighting and lack of employment opportunity are also experienced by them.

Dalit representatives also proffered some useful suggestions for overcoming problems faced by them in the panchayats. As Table 3.16 reveals, 36 per cent Dalits said that their problems should be heard by all concerned and attempts made to solve them, while 11 per cent said that without educating Dalits in general and Dalit representatives in

Table 3.16

Suggestions for overcoming problems of Dalit representatives: Sehore

S. No.	*Response*	*Dalit*		*Non-Dalit*	
		Frequency	*%*	*Frequency*	*%*
1.	No response	1	4	10	36
2.	Problems must be heard	10	36	5	18
3.	JP should solve problem	2	7	1	4
4.	Sarpanch should cooperate	I	4	-	-
5.	BPL list should be prepared Honestly	2	7	-	-
6.	People should be educated	3	11	5	18
7.	No difficulties faced	2	7	3	11
8.	Govt. should solve problems	I	4	2	7
9.	Mutual help can solve problems	-	-	1	4
10.	Dalit needs should be solved on priority basis	1	4	1	4
11.	Land/work opportunity should be provided	2	7	-	-
12.	2+3+4	3	11	-	-
	Total	28	100	28	100

particular, their problems cannot be solved. However, 7 per cent held that the Sarpanch should cooperate in resolving them, whereas others held that mutual help is required. A Dalit Panch of Bichia Panchayat argued, "General caste people do not allow us to speak. If I speak, I will invite trouble for me. Nobody listen to me because I am a Dalit. The government should constantly ask the non-Dalits to listen to our voice". Some respondents said that Janpad Panchayat members should come forward to solve their problems. Others were of the opinion that in order to strengthen the Dalit representatives, it is essential that the Dalit masses should be empowered. In this connection, a Dalit Panch of Thuna Kala Panchayat said that providing land could solve many of the problems as most arise out of poverty. "Near the forest area 750-800 acres of land are lying vacant. All the landless Dalits of my panchayat should be allotted up to 2.5 acres of land out of this land." Only 7 per cent of the Dalit respondents felt no problems. A significant number of non-Dalit respondents (36%) did not respond to this question but five of them are of the view that the problems of the Dalit representatives should be carefully heard, education should be popularized among them and all this should be done by the government through people's cooperation.

NGOs and Dalit Development

A number of NGOs are working in the sample area for the empowerment of Dalits, particularly in the remote rural and tribal areas. Some of them are effective because they know the area, understand the problems faced by Dalits and try to solve them with their cooperation. A good example is the 'Samartan' working in 127 panchayats in Sehore block, which has tried to strengthen the participatory development process through PRIs by increasing the participation of Dalits in the process of decentralization with informed decision-making capacities. Its activities have been in the areas of training at the village level, combined meetings of Mahila Mandals and Gram Sabha meetings to facilitate interaction between men and women, training of youth for capacity building for participation, 'mohalla' meetings prior to the Gram Sabha meetings to ensure quality discussion in the latter, NSS camps for students, providing information about panchayat meetings to all villagers, street plays to spread the message of participation among the villagers, SHGs (Self Help Groups) among women to help them financially, developing micro-plans for village development, literature on PRIs, meeting Dalit women specially Sarpanchas etc. The major aim has been to spread information and promote participation within the PRIs.

However, 68 per cent Dalit and 61 per cent non-Dalit respondents felt that the role of NGOs in the development of the Dalits is either ineffective or they are not in contact with the poor Dalit or non-Dalit masses. But six respondents said that in their area, the NGOs have not only constructed toilets but also launched literacy programme. Some of the respondents also reported that they have constructed bridges, toilets in school, organized training programmes, constructed school buildings and provided drainage facility. Thus, NGOs have undertaken construction works which help Dalits and non-Dalits but do not address the specific problems of social and cultural development of the former. Hence, many respondents felt that there is little difference between the work of the panchayats and NGOs. Therefore, respondents have made some suggestions for NGOs from the point of view of empowerment of the Dalit representatives in particular and the Dalit masses in general. Table 3.17 shows that rather than training programmes, both Dalit and non-Dalit respondents felt that NGOs should solve their problems or represent them before the government. Rather than financial help, Dalits are keen that NGOs should provide educational facilities, organize awareness programmes or carry out other concrete work for them which would help Dalit representatives to participate in the ongoing process of empowerment initiated by the government. The respondents also feel that both the organizations can work together as spokespersons and help in village development and more specifically for Dalits.

Table 3.17

NGOs and development of Dalits: Sehore

S. No.	*Response*	*Dalit*		*Non-Dalit*	
		Frequency	*%*	*Frequency*	*%*
1.	No response	3	11	7	25
2.	Training programme	-		1	4
3.	Solve their problem	4	14	4	14
4.	Present their demand before the government	3	11	1	4
5.	Concrete work should be done for them	2	7	4	14
6.	Financial help	-	-	1	4
7.	Education	3	11	2	7
8.	No NGO/no suggestion	1	4	1	4
9.	Awareness programme	2	7	5	18
10.	2+3+4	6	21	2	7
11.	3+4+5	4	14	-	-
	Total	28	100	28	100

Panchayat Functioning in Satna

In the present study, the level of awareness of respondents about ongoing rural development programmes under the panchayat was very low. Data presented in Table 3.18 depict that 75.51 per cent of the respondents did not know about ongoing programmes, only 12.24 per cent knew about them, while the rest had partial information about them. A majority of them accepted that they are not in a position to get any personal benefit from these programmes from the panchayat (Table 3.19). Thus, we find that majority of the Dalit members of the panchayat themselves have little or no information about programmes or expect any benefit from them and hence are not in a position to provide benefits to others in their community.

Table 3.18

Knowledge about programmes under the panchayat: Satna

Opinion	*No. of respondents*					
	Male		*Female*		*Total*	
	No.	*%*	*No.*	*%*	*No.*	*%*
Yes	5	10.20	01	2.04	06	12.24
No	20	40.81	17	34.69	37	75.51
Partially	6	12.24	-	-	06	12.24
Total	31	63.27	18	36.73	49	100

Table 3.19

Ability to get benefits of welfare and developmental projects: Satna

Opinion	*No. of respondents*					
	Male		*Female*		*Total*	
	No.	*%*	*No.*	*%*	*No.*	*%*
Yes	4	8.16	01	2.04	05	10.20
No	23	46.95	12	24.49	35	71.43
Partially	4	8.16	5	10.20	9	18.36
Total	31	63.27	18	36.73	49	100

Table 3.20

Knowledge about reservations in panchayats, government services and welfare schemes: Satna

Opinion	No. of respondents					
	Male		Female		Total	
	No.	%	No.	%	No.	%
Yes	07	(14.28)	01	(2.04)	08	(16.32)
No	24	(48.97)	17	(34.69)	41	(83.67)
Total	31	(63.27)	18	(36.73)	49	(100)

Table 3.21

Satisfaction with reservation policy: Satna

Opinion	No. of respondents					
	Male		Female		Total	
	No.	%	No.	%	No.	%
Yes	10	(20.40)	04	(8.16)	14	(28.57)
a. Because implementation is not right	03	(6.12)	02	(4.08)	05	(10.20)
No, if no reasons-						
b. Don't have information	18	(36.73)	12	(24.48)	30	(61.22)
Total	31	(63.27)	18	(36.73)	49	(100)

Table 3.22a

Knowledge about formation of the social justice Committee: Satna

Opinion	No. of respondents					
	Male		Female		Total	
	No.	%	No.	%	No.	%
Yes	05	(10.20)	01	(2.04)	06	(12.24)
No	26	(53.06)	17	(34.69)	43	(87.75)
Total	31	(63.27)	18	(36.73)	49	(100)

In fact, the vast majority of the Dalit leaders do not have any idea about affirmative action programmes of the government, reservation of seats, welfare programmes, etc. (Table 3.20). Most respondents are also not satisfied with the manner in which the reservation policy has been functioning at the level of the panchayat in their region. Here, 10.20 per cent feel that it is not implemented correctly while as much as 61.22 per cent do not have adequate information about the system (Table 3.21). And 87.75 per cent are not aware of the formation of the Social Justice Committee as part of the panchayat system (Table 3.22a). Table 3.22b shows that 59.18 per cent of the members pointed out that the committee is not functioning, 6.12 per cent said that sometimes meetings were held but some did not even know they were members and were not interested. Clearly, Dalits have not been able to make use of this provision in the PR system, which is meant to help them.

Table 3.22b

Role of Dalit member of the Social Justice Committee: Satna

Opinion	*No. of respondents*					
	Male		*Female*		*Total*	
	No.	*%*	*No.*	*%*	*No.*	*%*
Members don't take interest	02	4.08	-	-	02	4.08
Dalits got membership but they don't know about it	01	2.04	-	-	01	2.04
It's not functioning	18	36.73	11	22.44	29	59.18
It's OK	02	4.08	-		02	4.08
Sometimes meetings are arranged	01	2.04	02	4.08	03	6.12
No Response	07	14.28	05	10.20	12	24.48
Total	31	(63.27)	18	(36.73)	49	(100)

On being asked, what benefits they get from becoming a member of the panchayat, the respondents felt that it gave them knowledge about the structure and functions of the panchayat, provided them the experience of working with people belonging to different social and economic backgrounds and developed some capabilities of leadership. But, at the same time they also held that it created considerable pressure upon them, tension with persons belonging to other caste groups, political problems as they could not satisfy everyone, kept them away from their family and led to economic loss, as they had to give up time from their work. Table 3.23 reveals that over 75 per cent of the respondents have a cooperative relationship with people of their own caste, while only 12.24 per cent held they had such relationship with persons belonging to all caste groups. This affects the functioning of the panchayat. According to Table 3.24, 48.97 per cent of the Dalit respondents pointed out that they were able to provide leadership through decision-making in developmental programmes. However, 6.12 per cent of the female respondents admitted that they could do so only through the help of their husbands. Table 3.25 reveals that 83.79 per cent do not face the threat of a no-confidence motion either by Dalits or by any other person.

Table 3.23

With which caste/category respondents have cooperative relationship: Satna

Caste/Category	*No. of respondents*					
	Male		*Female*		*Total*	
	No.	*%*	*No.*	*%*	*No.*	*%*
Group of own caste	24	48.97	13	26.53	37	75.51
Others:						
a. General categories	2	4.08	3	6.12	5	10.20
b. Other backward classes	-	-	1	2.04	1	2.04
With every caste/category	5	10.20	1	2.04	6	12.24
Total	31	63.27	18	36.73	49	100

Table 3.24

Do you lead in developmental programmes: Satna

Caste/category	*No. of respondents*					
	Male		*Female*		*Total*	
	No.	*%*	*No.*	*%*	*No*	*%*
Yes	19	38.77	5	10.20	24	48.99
with the help of husband	-	-	3	6.12	3	6.12
No						
(a) due to lack of time	2	4.08	1	2.04	3	6.12
(b) never got opportunity	10	20.40	9	18.36	19	38.77
Total	31	63.27	18	36.37	49	100

Table 3.25

Did you face motion of no-confidence or such kind of threat: Satna

Caste/category	*No. of respondents*					
	Male		*Female*		*Total*	
	No.	*%*	*No.*	*%*	*No*	*%*
If yes, then,						
(a) by Dalits	-	-	1	2.04	1	2.04
(b) by non-Dalits	-	-	-	-	-	-
(c) by particular person	6	12.24	1	2.04	7	14.28
No	25	51.03	16	32.65	41	83.67
Total	31	63.27	18	36.73	49	100

Table 3.26

How do you feel if Dalit women contest for panchayat elections: Satna

Opinion	*No. of respondents*					
	Male		*Female*		*Total*	
	No.	*%*	*No.*	*%*	*No*	*%*
Appropriate	30	61.22	17	34.69	47	95.91
Inappropriate	-	-	-	-	-	-
Undecided	1	2.04	1	2.04	2	4.08
Total	31	63.27	18	36.73	49	100

Table 3.27

Are women confined to the home and husbands take all the decisions: Satna

Opinion	No. of respondents					
	Male		Female		Total	
	No.	%	No.	%	No.	%
Yes	23	(46.94)	9	(18.36)	32	(65.30)
No	8	(16.32)	9	(18.36)	17	(34.69)
Total	31	(63.27)	18	(36.73)	49	(100.00)

Table 3.28

Women's participation in the panchayat: Satna

Opinion	No. of respondents					
	Male		Female		Total	
	No.	%	No.	%	No.	%
Self	28	(57.14)	17	(34.69)	45	(91.83)
Husband	2	(4.08)	-		2	(4.08)
Others	-		-		-	
Meeting is not held	1	(2.04)	-		1	(2.04)
Don't participate	-		1	(2.04)	1	(2.04)
Total	31	(63.27)	18	(36.73)	49	(100.00)

Women, particularly Dalit women, have only recently entered into the new panchayats. The attitude of the respondents regarding the participation of women in panchayats is positive but skeptical about their abilities to undertake the tasks given to them. Table 3.26 exhibits that 95 per cent of the respondents felt that Dalit women should contest elections. But, at the same time, 65.30 per cent pointed out that women at present are confined to domestic activities and it is their husbands who actually take the decisions in the panchayat (Table 3.27). The reason given was that they are not able to handle the tasks assigned to them. But, the large majority agreed that women do physically attend panchayat meetings and are gradually learning to participate and only 4.08 per cent held that their husbands represented them. About 34.69 per cent of the women stated that they represented themselves and did not need the support of their husbands (Table 3.28).

Table 3.29

Respondents' participation in meetings: Satna

Opinion	*No. of respondents*					
	Male		*Female*		*Total*	
	No.	*%*	*No.*	*%*	*No.*	*%*
Yes	22	(44.89)	11	(22.45)	33	(67.35)
No reasons:						
(a) Lack of time	1	(2.04)	-	-	1	(2.04)
(b) Lack of awareness	-	-	-	-	-	-
(c) Inconvenient time of meetings	-	-	-	-	-	-
(d) Meeting place is far away	-	-	-	-	-	-
(e) Lack of interest	2	(4.08)	2	(4.08)	4	(8.16)
(f) No information about meetings	-	-	-	-	-	-
(i) Quarrel and pressure	1	(2.04)	-	-	1	(2.04)
(e+f)	1	(2.04)	-	-	1	(2.04)
(d+f)	-	-	1	(2.04)	1	(2.04)
(a+b+e)	-	-	3	(6.12)	3	(6.12)
(a+c+e)	1	(2.04)	-	-	1	(2.04)
(a+b+e+f)	3	(6.12)	-	-	3	(6.12)
(b+c+e+f)	-	-	1	(2.04)	1	(2.04)
Total	31	(63.27)	18	(36.73)	49	(100)

The study also revealed that participation in the meetings of the panchayat is fairly high but not very productive or meaningful for most respondents. Majority of the respondents (67.35%) participate in meetings of the panchayat, 2.04 per cent held that they cannot spare the time, 8.18 per cent lack interest, 2.04 per cent, said that there is a quarrelsome environment in the meetings, and a similar number, i.e., 2.04 per cent pointed to lack of information about the meeting (Table 3.29). However, 14.28 per cent of the respondents admitted that they go for meetings but sit idly (inactively), 6.12 per cent said that most of the time meetings get cancelled due to dispute, 8.16 per cent said that there is lack of freedom in meetings, 8.16 per cent said that they do not get cooperation and 4.08 per cent said that after a few meetings now they do not go (Table 3.30). An important reason for lack of interest or inability to participate properly is that an overwhelming majority of the leaders did not get any training as panchayat representatives (Table 3.31).

Table 3.30

How do respondents feel during meeting: Satna

Opinion	*No. of respondents*					
	Male		*Female*		*Total*	
	No.	*%*	*No.*	*%*	*No.*	*%*
Yes	22	(44.89)	11	(22.45)	33	(67.35)
Normal	13	(26.53)	07	(14.28)	20	(40.82)
Excited	05	(10.20)	01	(2.04)	06	(12.24)
Uncomfortable	01	(2.04)	02	(4.08)	03	(6.12)
Inactive participation						
Meetings get	02	(4.08)	05	(10.20)	07	(14.28)
Cancelled due to dispute	02	(4.08)	01	(2.04)	03	(6.12)
Lack of freedom in meetings	03	(6.12)	01	(2.04)	04	(8.16)
They don't get cooperation	04	(8.16)	-	-	04	(8.16)
Now don't go in meetings	01	(2.04)	01	(2.04)	02	(4.08)
Total	31	(63.27)	18	(36.73)	49	(100)

Table 3.31

Did you get any training after being elected as panchayat representative: Satna

Opinion	*No. of respondents*					
	Male		*Female*		*Total*	
	No.	*%*	*No.*	*%*	*No.*	*%*
Yes	4	(8.16)	2	(4.08)	6	(12.24)
No	27	(55.1)	16	(32.65)	43	(87.76)
Total	31	(63.27)	18	(36.73)	49	(100.00)

Table 3.32

Do officials face any kind of problem in working with PR system: Satna

Opinion	*No.*	*%*
Yes	11	50
No	11	50
Total	22	100

Table 3.33

Officials' perception of the kinds of problems faced by Dalits due to reservation in PR: Satna

Kinds of Problems	*No.*	*%*
Able persons are not getting benefit and intelligent persons are not able to get leadership	2	9.09
Due to reservation illiterate and unaware persons got elected who could not get benefit from government	4	18.18
Due to reservation those persons got elected whose population is less than others, so others get unsatisfied	2	9.09
Women got elected due to reservation, while they work as a dummy of their husband or other persons.	2	9.09
Representative of reserved categories work under pressure of non-Dalits	2	9.09
No problem	10	45.45
Total	22	100.00

Table 3.32 shows that 50 per cent of the respondents selected from the panchayat officials in the sample held that they face problems in the working of the panchayat due to faulty rules and interference by the government etc. While 95.45 per cent of the respondents among the officials held that reservation in PRIs is an appropriate step, at least half felt that it is not effective. They pointed out that reservations in many cases do not help the Dalits as they are illiterate, lack capability or work under pressure from the non-Dalits and Dalit women as proxy for their husbands (Table 3.33). Table 3.34 demonstrates that panchayat officials pointed out have also differences

in the capabilities of Dalits and non-Dalits which affect the manner in which they function in the panchayats. A majority of Dalits are not aware or those who are aware are not elected. Besides, they lack education, are not efficient, face tremendous pressure, do not get public cooperation and are economically too weak to be able to make a mark in the functioning of the panchayats. Due to these, they are hesitant and dependent and incapable of making a decision independently. Dalits also do not get honour or appreciation for work well done; rather, they face insults, which affect their functioning adversely. Though, most officials accepted that PR system is now working better, majority of them also suggested reforms in the existing system such as giving education preference in reservation, greater decentralization of power leading to formulation of schemes at Gram Sabha level, raising the awareness of the rural population

Table 3.34

Differences between Dalit and non-Dalit leaderships according to panchayat officials: Satna

Non-Dalit leadership	*Dalit leadership*	*No.*	*%*
Self aware	Not aware, and who are aware, can not be elected	2	9.09
Work efficiently	Lack of efficiency	2	9.09
Get cooperation of public, there is no pressure	Don't get cooperation of public and face pressures	3	13.64
Have good understanding due to education	Academically and economically weak	2	9.09
Capable of taking decisions freely	Hesitant in taking decisions and dependency on other	1	4.55
Get appreciation and honour	Get insulted, which affect their functioning	1	4.55
Implement government scheme effectively	Find them weak and under pressure	1	4.55
No difference	No difference	5	22.73
Didn't get such experience	No difference	5	22.73
Total		22	100.00

of their rights and duties in the panchayat, providing value education to representatives, reform in the rules of the panchayats to improve functioning, giving panchayats the right of imposing penalty and punishment (Tables 3.35 and 3.36).

Table 3.35

Officials' perception whether PR is achieving its objectives: Satna

Opinion	*No.*	*%*
Yes	20	90.90
No	2	13.64
Total	22	100.00

Table 3.36

Officials' perception of scope for reform in PR and reservation system: Satna

Opinion	*No.*	*%*
Yes	13	59.09
No	9	40.90
Total	22	100.00

As Table 3.37 shows that caste plays a role in the relationship between panchayat members and the panchayat officials although other factors are also significant. Non-Dalit respondents enjoy a much better relationship with the panchayat officials – both Dalit and non-Dalit – than the Dalit respondents and are able to get their work done more easily. In contrast, Dalit respondents enjoy a better relationship with Dalit than with non-Dalit panchayat officials. And 24.89 per cent of the Dalit respondents felt that their relationship with Dalit panchayat officials was normal, 55.10 per cent felt it to be good and 8.16 per cent not good. In contrast, only 18.36 per cent Dalit respondents had good relationship with non-Dalit officials, 44.88 per cent had normal, 8.16 per cent not good and

28.57 per cent had no relationship with panchayat officials. As much as 32.65 per cent of the Dalit respondents said that they had no relationship with the Dalit panchayat officials and 28.75 per cent with the non-Dalit officials, which points to lack of interest on the part of the bureaucracy. On the other hand, 55.10 per cent of the non-Dalit leaders held that they enjoyed a good relationship with Dalit panchayat officials, whereas only 8.16 per cent held that their relationship was not good. In case of non-Dalit officials, 57.14 per cent of the non-Dalit respondents have good relationship, 36.61 per cent have normal, 6.12 per cent not good and 6.12 have no relationship (Table 3.38).

Table 3.37

What kind of relationship do respondents have with panchayat officials in the opinion of non-Dalits: Satna

Type of relationship	*No. of respondents*					
	Male		*Female*		*Total*	
	No.	*%*	*No.*	*%*	*No.*	*%*
If respondent is Dalit:						
a. Good	21	42.86	6	12.24	27	55.10
b. Normal	10	20.41	2	4.08	12	24.89
c. Not good	2	4.08	2	4.08	4	8.16
d. No relationship	2	4.08	2	4.08	4	8.16
e. No Dalit officials	2	4.08	-	-	2	4.08
If respondent is non-Dalit:						
a. Good	24	48.98	4	8.16	28	57.14
b. Normal	11	22.44	4	8.16	15	36.61
c. Not good	1	2.04	2	4.08	3	6.12
d. No relationship	1	2.04	2	4.08	3	6.12

Table 3.38

What kind of relationship do respondents have with panchayat officials in the opinion of Dalits: Satna

Type of relationship	*No. of respondents*					
	Male		*Female*		*Total*	
	No.	*%*	*No.*	*%*	*No.*	*%*
If respondent is Dalit:						
a. Good	8	16.33	4	8.16	12	24.89
b. Normal	11	22.44	6	12.24	17	34.68
c. Not good	4	8.16	-	-	4	8.16
d. No relationship	8	16.33	8	16.33	16	32.65
e. No Dalit officials	-	-	-	-	-	-
If respondent is non-Dalit:						
a. Good	5	10.20	4	8.16	9	18.36
b. Normal	14	28.57	8	16.33	22	44.88
c. Not good	4	8.16	-	-	4	8.16
d. No relationship	8	16.33	6	12.24	14	28.57

Problems Faced by Dalit Members

As in Sehore Panchayat, Dalit members of Satna panchayat also face a number of problems, which do not allow them to function effectively. They agree that most of these stem from their illiteracy and inexperience. Among the respondents – mostly male – said that they faced problems after being elected. Table 3.39 reveals that 53.06 per cent of the non-Dalit respondents agreed that most Dalit members are not free to take decisions but are the 'dummy' of the powerful 'upper caste' persons in the village, i.e., Dalit candidates are supported financially by non-Dalits during the election and afterwards are expected to function according to their dictates. The table further points out that 71.43 per cent of the non-Dalit respondents held that Dalit leaders function as dummy of non-Dalits. Similarly, cooperation with other caste groups is necessary to be able to participate meaningfully in the panchayat. But, as Table 3.40 makes it clear, only 12.24 per cent of the Dalits have a cooperative relationship with people of every caste or category, 75.51 per cent with people of their own caste, and only 2.04 per cent with people belonging to the OBC category.

Table 3.39

Sometimes Dalit candidates function as a dummy of non-Dalits: Satna

Opinion	No. of respondents					
	Male		Female		Total	
	No.	%	No.	%	No.	%
True	19	38.78	7	14.29	26	53.06
Not true	6	12.24	4	8.16	10	20.40
Never true	5	10.20	3	6.12	8	16.33
Not known	1	2.04	4	8.16	5	10.20
Total	31	63.27	18	36.73	49	100.00

Table 3.40

With which caste/category respondents have cooperative relationship: Satna

Opinion	No. of respondents					
	Male		Female		Total	
	No.	%	No.	%	No.	%
Group of own caste	24	48.97	13	26.53	37	75.51
Others:						
a general categories	2	4.08	3	6.12	5	10.20
b. other backward classes	-	-	1	2.04	1	2.04
With every caste/ category	5	10.20	1	2.04	6	12.24
Total	31	63.27	18	36.73	49	100.00

For these reasons, many Dalit representatives feel that without reservation no Dalit can win an election due to the prevailing power structure. About half the Dalit Sarpanchas said that the previous Sarpanch was not cooperative with them, while others pointed out that they are often blackmailed by Dalits.

However, a section of the respondents was more positive and held that things are changing and Dalits are now becoming more aware and capable and will be able to get out of the grip of the upper caste/class section of the village.

Table 3.41

Do respondents find them capable of fulfilling needs and aspirations of their community: Satna

Opinion	*No. of respondents*					
	Male		*Female*		*Total*	
	No.	*%*	*No.*	*%*	*No.*	*%*
Yes:						
a. by majority	17	34.69	12	24.49	29	59.18
b. by self decision if don't get majority	-	-	-	-	-	-
c. above both	01	2.04	-	-	01	2.04
No:						
a. Due to lack of time	03	6.12	-	-	03	6.12
b. due to non-cooperation of panchayat representatives and officials	07	14.28	2	4.08	09	18.37
c. due to lack of information and awareness	01	2.04	4	8.16	05	10.20
d. They are not able to function due to risk and pressure	02	4.08	-	-	02	4.08
Total	31	63.27	18	36.73	49	100

Table 3.42

Do you feel, if you belong to rich class or non-Dalit then decisions taken shall be more effective: Satna

Opinion	*No. of respondents*					
	Male		*Female*		*Total*	
	No.	*%*	*No.*	*%*	*No.*	*%*
Yes	29	59.18	18	36.73	47	95.92
No	2	4.08	-	-	2	4.08
Total	31	63.27	18	36.73	49	100.00

Table 3.43

Are Dalit Sarpanch capable of fulfilling ambitions, needs and desires of non-Dalits: Satna

Opinion	No. of Respondents					
	Male		Female		Total	
	No.	%	No.	%	No.	%
Yes:	6	42.86	1	7.14	7	50
No:						
(a) They work as per their wish	1	7.14	-	-	1	7.14
(b) Gram Sabha meetings are not successful due to jealous	2	14.28	-	-	2	14.28
(c) They have caste feelings don't have good relation with non-Dalits	1	7.14	1	7.14	2	14.28
(d) They are in pressure	2	14.28	-	-	2	14.28
Total	12	85.71	2	14.28	14	100

Among the respondents, 59.18 per cent of the Dalit leaders held that they are capable of fulfilling needs and aspirations of their community, if they receive their support in the panchayat, when decisions are made. However, 6.12 per cent respondents complained that they are not able to fulfil the needs and aspirations of their community due to lack of time as they are busy in earning their livelihood, 18.37 per cent say that they do not get cooperation of panchayat representatives and officials, 10.20 per cent agree that they lack information and awareness and 4.08 per cent agree that they are not able to function due to risk and pressure (Table 3.41). Table 3.42 indicates the pressures under which Dalits operate within the panchayats. Among them, 95.92 per cent felt that if they were rich, and 38.78 per cent felt that if they were not dependent for their livelihood upon non-Dalits, they would be able to function much more effectively in the panchayat. This points to the power structure within the panchayat that determines to a large extent its functioning. On the other hand, 50 per cent of non-Dalit respondents accept that Dalit Sarpanchas are able to fulfil ambitions, needs and desires of non-Dalits, 7.14 per cent feel that they work as per their wish, 14.28 per cent say that due to jealousy work does not get done, 14.28 per cent say that they do not have good relations with non-Dalits and 14.28 per cent say that they are always in pressure, which does not allow them to function properly (Table 3.43).

Table 3.44

What should be done to improve functioning of Dalit leadership in panchayats: Satna

Opinion	*No. of Respondents*					
	Male		*Female*		*Total*	
	No.	*%*	*No.*	*%*	*No.*	*%*
Dalits should be educated or those Dalits who are educated and able should be elected. So facilities for education should be improved.	05	(10.20)	03	(6.12)	08	(16.32)
Implemented reservation system and provisions are O.K., only administrations system should be disciplined so that the last man could be benefited.	03	(6.12)	02	(4.08)	05	(10.20)
Rules should be strict and they should be given more power.	02	(4.08)	01	(2.04)	03	(6.12)
Dalits should be given land for agriculture and house, their development should be considered so that they could be empowered and function effectively. They should be made self-dependent.	1	(2.04)	2	(4.08)	3	(6.12)
Awareness program should be introduced so that people can get benefit of programs.	4	(4.16)	1	(2.04)	5	(10.20)
Some of the benefits and cash amount should be provided to Dalits directly.	2	(4.08)	-	-	2	(4.08)
Reservation on the basis of the caste should be removed because due to this they face discrimination.	2	(4.08)	-	-	2	(4.08)
Not know	12	(24.48)	09	(18.36)	21	(42.85)
Total	31	(63.27)	18	(36.73)	49	(100)

Mere election is not sufficient condition to work for the people. And 42.86 per cent of the Dalit respondents said that they are not able to function properly due to various constraints, while 65.31 per cent non-Dalit respondents are able to function properly. Many respondents pointed out that Dalit representatives elected for the first time lack confidence and capacity to function as Sarpanchas particularly whenever large budgets involving construction have to be handled. Around 43 per cent of the Dalit respondents could not provide suggestions on how to improve their functioning (Table 3.44). But, the other respondents suggested a number of measures such as education to Dalits, awareness about rules and regulations, implementation of reservation policy, land to Dalits etc.

Conclusion

MP has a large Dalit population in its northern districts. The state has also witnessed some improvement over the last two decades that has helped Dalits. Literacy rates are rising among the weaker sections. However, the state continues to have an oppressive social structure, which does not allow Dalits to make full use of the reservations provided in the 73rd Constitutional Amendment Act. While the BSP has a presence, particularly in the northern districts, it has not undertaken mobilization as in UP. Consequently, social and political awareness remains low and Dalits are unable to question the hold that the upper and middle castes still have on the panchayats. Dalit women, despite being elected to the panchayats, continue to suffer on both the counts of caste and gender.

However, during the 1990s, some change has taken place, the impact of which on Dalits is not yet visible. It has yet to be translated into public action on the part of the Dalits. As our field study shows, many of them are unhappy about the working of the panchayats and the social position they occupy in the village structure. It is a matter of time that they will be able to look after their own interests and participate in local governance. A distinct characteristic of MP is the large number of NGOs, which are working among the weaker sections trying to get them land, assets, education etc. This will also help the Dalits to overcome the problems they face in working in the new panchayats. However, MP does show that provision of reservations alone cannot help Dalits and much more is needed to make them capable of using their position in the new panchayats to introduce change which will be beneficial to them and to society as a whole.

5

Dalit Leadership in Panchayats in Haryana

A Case Study of Kalanaur (Rohtak)

Haryana has a distinct status among the four states under the present study due to its economic development but low socio-cultural advancement. It lags behind Himachal Pradesh in terms of literacy and status of women but is ahead in terms of agricultural and industrial advancement, if compared to all other states of the study. The state of Haryana is situated between 27'3' to 31'9' N latitude and 74'5' to 77'6' E longitude. It lies in the plains between the basins of the rivers Indus and Ganga. It has an area of just about 44,212 square kilometres. The state's landscapes and soil fertility are remarkably diverse, i.e., from the lower Shiwaliks in the north to the Aravali hills in the south. In between lies the fertile land. The Yamuna river forms a natural boundary between UP and Haryana.

Haryana is the most developed among the states undertaken for the present study. It has also implemented a new industrial policy, which echoes the commitment of the liberalization policy. It has witnessed rapid growth of its economy – both in agriculture and industry. The Green Revolution has made a significant impact in the agricultural field. Though, there is improvement in the economic status of the people in general, being a feudal and patriarchal society, the state of Haryana still lags behind in terms of Human Development Index. The sex ratio in the state is low. The status of women is very low with the *purdah* system still in vogue even in the urban areas.

In order to conduct the present study on Dalit leadership in panchayats, it was decided to select Rohtak district of the state, which has the largest concentration of literate Scheduled Caste (SC) population (57.79%). The district recorded the highest percentage of literate population in 1991 as against 39.22 per cent of the state average. The Rohtak tehsil has 18.26 per cent of SC population. Kalanaur block, which has a relatively largest concentration of SC population, was selected for the present study. Another reason to select Kalanaur block of Rohtak was the fact of its being a reserved assembly constituency. The study in Haryana clubbed Dalit and non-Dalit leadership with a focus on Dalit issues in general. It enables us to test whether economic development undermines the caste-based inequalities and how the new leadership responds to Dalit issues.

Haryana suffers from a democratic deficit. Though, Rohtak and adjoining districts are economically developed, they have witnessed the commission of worst kind of atrocities on Dalits in a big way. Recently, in Gohana town, in the adjoining district of Sonepat, a Dalit locality was put on fire by the dominant Jat caste. In another district Jhajjar, when four Dalits were spotted with a dead cow and were handed over to the police post of Dulina in the evening on 15th of October 2003, they were murdered by the people of so-called high caste. In spite of media pressure and the persuasive appeal by political parties such as the BSP and the Congress, the 'Khap' panchayats of the higher caste mobilized the masses warning the state not to take any action against those involved and identified in killing the Dalit youth.

In another incident, Karan Singh, a Dalit Sarpanch was asked to attend a meeting on October 12, 2003 and did not return home. The mysterious circumstances, in which the Sarpanch of Pehrawar village of Sampla block in Rohtak district disappeared, are quite surprising. The villagers and Dalits believe highhandedness and feudal mindsets, which subjected the Dalit Sarpanch to suffer on account of oppressed measures, adopted by certain group of people belonging to high caste. The aggrieved family got the support of certain Dalit organizations and left parties but the state has not responded so far in this case. Still efforts are on by the National Commission for SCs and STs on the Haryana government to enquire about the missing Dalit Sarpanch.

In one of the villages under study, Masudpur, which has less than 10 per cent of Dalit population, four women and one youth of Dalit community were attacked by some members of high caste people for not having supported one of the high caste candidates for the post of Sarpanch in last election. It is somewhat disconcerting to note that the attack on them occurred after three years of the election, i.e., on 7th of March 2003, on the pretext of some dispute that arose in the cricket match. Thus, it is somewhat a common feature for the members of the high caste people to humiliate and attack Dalits on one pretext or the other. This shows the deepest caste mentality that works against Dalits.

Rohtak district has five blocks, namely, Rohtak, Meham, Kalanaur, Lakhanmajra and Sampla. Since Kalanaur block was selected for the purpose of the present study, all the twelve villages, consisting of six Dalit and non-Dalit Sarpanchas each, represented the typical characteristics of Kalanaur block. Out of the six Dalit-headed villages, three, namely, Anwal, Lahli and Patwapur, had female Sarpanchas and three others, namely, Nigana, Kahnaur and Temurpur, had male Sarpanchas. Six other non-Dalit-headed villages included three women and men Sarpanchas each. Three non-Dalit women Sarpanchas were from Sangahera, Jindran and Gudhan, while three villages headed by male Sarpanchas were Masudpur, Khedadi and Madodhi Radhyan. Out of a total of 127 Panchas from these twelve villages, 109 were interviewed and data was collected with the help of interview schedule. A group interview in Dalit-headed panchayats namely, Anwal, Patwapur and Nigana, was also conducted to elicit the opinion of the people about Dalit leaders' effective functioning in the panchayats. Some key informants were also interviewed to ascertain their views about the functioning of Dalit leaders.

Haryana has 6,059 Gram Panchayats but the second successive election which was held in the year 2000 for the local bodies consisted of 6,020 Gram Panchayats only as the elections for 39 Gram Panchayats were not held until 2001 (see Table A). And, therefore, the figures given here do not include those 39 panchayats. What is remarkable to note is the fact that for the first time in the history of panchayat elections, it was noticed that the members belonging to the SC group and women were actively participating in the election process. It has given them a feeling that they are also part of the government.

Table A

Members of Gram Panchayat elected in 1999-2000

State/ Distt./ Block	*No. of Gram Panchayats*	*Men*			*Women*			*BC*	*Total*
		Gen.	*SC*	*Total*	*Gen.*	*SC*	*Total*		
Haryana	6020	25245 (46.38)	7597 (13.95)	30842 (56.66)	13728 (25.22)	4211 (7.73)	17939 (32.96)	5644 (10.37)	54425
Rohtak	151	830 (45.98)	232 (12.85)	1062 (58.83)	467 (25.87)	135 (7.47)	602 (33.35)	141 (7.81)	1805
Kalanaur	24	11 (45.83)	4 (16.66)	16 (66.66)	5 (20.83)	3 (12.5)	8 (33.33)	-	24

Note: Figures in parenthesis show percentage.

Source: Statistical Abstract of Haryana, 1999-2000, Economic and Statistical Organization, Planning Department, Government of Haryana, 2001: 650-651.

It is clear from the above table that adequate representation in panchayats has been accorded to both SCs and women, who were so far not represented in traditional panchayat system. In Rohtak also adequate representation to both Dalits men and women have been given as per the constitutional provision. Representation of SC males in Rohtak panchayats was 12.85 per cent, while for female it was 7.47 per cent. In Kalanaur block also male SC Panchas constituted 16.66 per cent, while SC women constituted 12.5 per cent. It is somewhat remarkable to note that in Kheradi village, an SC Sarpanch was elected from general seat, which clearly indicates that the SCs by virtue of their numerical strength may dominate the political scene in times to come.

It is significant to mention here that Kheradi village had 54.65 per cent of SC population and due to the numerical preponderance of SC population, it was a little easier for the SC candidate to successfully contest election against non-SC candidate even from the general seat. The Sarpanch, who belonged to Dhanak caste, is a young graduate and by virtue of being young, dynamic, enthusiastic and educated, he could manage to win the election even as a general candidate. There was no stiff opposition. Thus, numerical strength holds key for a candidate to win the election. The numerical preponderance, combined with economic well-being and education, accounts for the decisive dominance of the SCs in elections. It is pertinent to mention here that for SC candidate, it is not possible to win assembly seat from unreserved constituency. And, in this sense, the panchayat election at village level favouring SC candidate from a general seat is quite exceptional and noteworthy.

Population Structure and Social Characteristics of the Studied Villages

In the studied villages, the most populous village was Kahnaur which had a population of 7,611 (Tables 4.5 and 4.6). No wonder, the maximum number of panchayat members came from this village. The village as such had 10 of its panchayat members belonging to upper caste groups, three to Jats, two to

Brahmins and five to Khatris and Aroras. Next to the high caste groups, the village had eight SC members as Panchas. Next populous village in our sample was Nigana with a total strength of 4,886. While Kahnaur had majority of its panchayat members representing upper castes, Nigana had none. Nigana had Mir Singh, who came from Balmiki caste and was elected Sarpanch. Along with him the village had four Panchas from Chamar caste group and three from Balmiki caste group. Among the Dalit-headed panchayats, Temurpur was the most sparsely populated village with a total population of 420 only.

The distribution of male-female population in the studied villages also gives an evidence of the fact that in Kalanaur block, specially in all the Dalit-headed villages, the deficit of female population was not all that sharp as one notices in case of the state average, which was recorded 861 in 2001. For Rohtak district, it was recorded 847 in 2001. The data, however, for the studied villages belong to 1991 census, but the data on village population indicate the sharp variation that exists at the village level. According to the census enumeration for 2001, sex ratio for Rohtak was 861, in Meham block it was 865, while in Kalanaur block it was 883. Thus, it is clear from Table 4.7 that both in Rohtak district (74.56%) and Kalanaur block (76.83%), the literacy rate (68.59%) was much above the state average, but the figures for SC population, specially its literacy percentage, showed tremendous gap in Rohtak district for males and females. The general literacy level for males and females was 84.29 per cent and 63.19 per cent showing a gap of 21 per cent.

So far as the sex ratio in the studied villages of Dalit-headed panchayats is concerned, the deficit of females against males was not as sharp as one finds at the state and district levels. In fact, in Temurpur village, as against 28 SC males (6.66%), there were 58 females (13.80%) and that shows an exceptional situation. This kind of situation is normally true of state like Kerala where the male-female ratio is quite positive (1,036 females per 1,000 males). There existed a sharp gap in the literacy figure for the studied villages between males and females. In Nigana, for example, the male literacy figure recorded 34.60 per cent population, while female SC literacy rate is incredibly low with 1.14 per cent only. In Lahli, Patwapur and Kahnaur also, the SCs female literacy was 50 per cent less than the male. In Lahli, it was 15.47 per cent as against male's 34.22 per cent, while in Patwapur, it was 16.18 per cent as against male's 32.06 and in Kalanaur, it was 17.51 per cent for females and 34.33 per cent for males (see Table 4.5). In Dalit-headed village, male literacy on an average was 33.61 while female literacy recorded an average of 15.50. That means the gap between male and female literacy was 18.11 per cent.

As regards the population of the studied villages of non-Dalit headed panchayats, Gudhan was the largest village with a population of 3,358. Here also, the shortage of female was quite striking. For the entire Kalanaur block, the sex ratio was 883. The studied villages also showed a deficit of 79 males per 100 population. That meant, it was slightly better than the sex ratio recorded at the block level. There was, however, a growing trend towards getting the sex of the baby detected in the womb with a purpose of aborting female foetus and retaining male foetus. Both in Anwal and Patwapur, where we had a group discussion and detailed in-depth interview with the Sarpanchas, both the female Sarpanchas expressed their inability to do anything about it.

The present study on Dalit and non-Dalit leaders in Haryana panchayats of Rohtak district is confined to Kalanaur block, which has 24 Gram Sabhas. As per the constitutional provision, one/third, i.e., eight Gram Sabhas had women Sarpanchas and out of them, three were elected from reserved seats and five from general seats. Anwal, Patwapur and Lahli had female Dalit Sarpanchas. Patwapur has the largest concentration of SC population (44.70%), followed by Lahli with (36.95%) and Anwal with (34.87%). Situation, however, was different in rest of 16 Gram Sabhas, which were represented by male Sarpanchas. Here, Kahnaur, Nigana and Temurpur are the reserved seats for SCs with Katesara as yet another reserved seat for BC. There is one general seat in Kheradi village from where an SC Sarpanch was elected. Thus, besides three SC seats, one seat of general category had also been captured by the SC candidate.

Profile of the Elected Representatives

Caste profile of elected representatives in Dalit-headed panchayats reveals that out of 126 panchayat members belonging to high caste groups, Jat, Khatri and Arora (Punjabi) and Brahmin did not constitute majority. Their total number was only 28, i.e., 22.22 per cent of the total Panchas in twelve villages (see Table 4.1). Among the high castes Khatri and Arora belonging to the Punjabi community had dominant position with 18 in number. Jat Panchas were five and Brahmins were just three in number. The Panchas belonging to the middle castes, i.e., Khati, Lohar and Chhippi constituted seven in total (5.51%). It was interesting to note that the numerical strength of SC Panchas was conspicuous with 35 in number, which consisted of 27.55 per cent of the total. But, here again, the Chamars were in a dominant position with 23 (18.25%). They are the single caste group from within SC groups, which has such a decisive dominance so far as their representation in Gram Panchayat is concerned. Next to Chamar is Balmiki whose number is 6 (nearly 5%). Even the profile of Sarpanchas so far as their caste background was concerned in Anwal, Lahli, Kahnaur and Temurpur, belonged to the Chamar, while both in Patwapur and Nigana the female Sarpanchas, belonged to Balmiki caste.

The situation in non-Dalit-headed panchayats was somewhat varied. Among the high caste group, the representation of Jat was quite conspicuous. Punjabi, Khatri and Arora castes also had decisive presence. The overall strength of Panchas, out of a total of 126 was 29, which is about 22.83 per cent. The number of middle caste Panchas was 9 in total with 7.08 per cent, but it was Dalit representation with 17 in number

(13.38%), which was quite significant to note (see Tables 4.1 and 4.2).

Table 4.1

Caste-wise representation of Panchas in Dalit-headed villages: Kalanaur

Caste	*Dalit-headed villages*						
	Anwal	*Lahli*	*Patwa-pur*	*Nigana*	*Kahn-aur*	*Temur-pur*	*Total*
Jat	1	-	3	-	3	-	5 (3.96)
Brahmin	-	-	1	-	2	-	3 (2.38)
Khatri and Arora	5	4	1	-	5	3	18 (14.28)
Rajput	-	1	-	-	-	-	1 (0.79)
Bania	-	1	-	-	-	-	1 (0.79)
Yadav	-	-	-	-	-	-	-
Upper castes							28 (22.22)
Khati	-	-	-	-	1	-	1 (0.79)
Lohar	1	1	-	-	1	-	3 (2.38)
Kumhar	-	-	1	-	-	-	1 (0.79)
Chhippi	-	-	-	1	-	-	1 (0.79)
Bharbhuja	1	1	-	-	-	-	2 (1.58)
Gurjar	-	-	-	-	1	-	1 (0.79)
Jogi	-	-	-	-	-	1	1 (0.79)
Bairagi	-	-	-	-	-	-	-
Middle castes							10 (7.93)
Chamar	4	4	3	4	5	3	23 (18.25)
Bhangi	1	-	-	-	-	-	1 (0.79)
Balmiki	-	1	2	3	-	-	6 (4.76)
Dhanak	1	-	-	-	1	1	2 (1.58)
OD	-	-	-	-	2	-	2 (1.58)
Lower castes							34 (26.98)

Note: Figures in parenthesis show percentage.

Table 4.2

Caste-wise representation of Panchas in non-Dalit-headed villages: Kalanaur

Caste	Non-Dalit-headed villages							
	Sanga-hera	*Jind-ran*	*Gud-han*	*Masud-pur*	*Kher-adi*	*Mada-udi Radh-iyan*	*Total*	*Grand Total*
Jat	-	4	7	-	1	1	13	18
Brahmin	1	-	-	4	-	-	5	8
Khatri and Arora	5	1	-	-	1	1	8	26
Rajput	-	-	-	-	-	-	-	1
Bania	-	-	-	-	-	-	-	1
Yadav	-	-	-	-	-	1	1	1
Upper castes							27	55
Khati	-	-	1	-	-	-	1	2
Lohar	1	1	1	-	1	1	5	8
Kumhar	-	1	1	1	-	1	4	5
Chhippi	-	-	-	-	-	-	-	1
Bharbhuja	-	-	-	-	-	-	-	2
Gurjar	-	-	-	-	-	-	-	1
Jogi	-	-	-	-	-	-	-	1
Bairagi	-	1	-	-	-	-	1	1
Middle castes							20	21
Chamar	1	1	-	1	2	3	8	31
Bhangi	-	-	-	-	-	-	-	1
Balmiki	-	-	-	-	-	1	1	7
Dhanak	1	-	2	-	3	-	6	8
OD	-	-	-	-	1	-	1	3
Lower castes								50

It was interesting to find that among the non-Dalit-headed panchayats in Sangahera and Masudpur, Sarpanchas were females belonging to Brahmin caste groups. In Jindran, the female Sarpanch was Bairagi, which is categorized under OBC group and in Gudhan the male Sarpanch was a Jat, which is recognized as the dominant caste of Haryana. In Madaudi Radhyan, the male Sarpanch was Yadav, while in Kheradi the Sarpanch was Dhanak, which is categorized as an SC Thus, it is clear from the caste profile that majority of the upper caste Panchas belonged to Khatri and Arora and next to it were Jats and Brahmins. The middle caste representation was less in comparison to SC and upper caste groups. Their total strength was 20 in number, i.e., 15.87 per cent as against the middle caste groups the members belonging to the SC group was also quite pronounced. They constituted 39.68 per cent of the total. Within the SC group, the strength of Chamars was quite pronounced. Next to Chamars, Dhanaks and Balmikis had their representation with 8 and 7 respectively.

As regards the family background of the Panchas, majority of them came from the nuclear family background (see Tables 4.3 and 4.4). The Panchas belonging to the nuclear family background were less in Nigana and Gudhan. Their total strength was 71, which is 65.13 per cent. The panchayat members who belonged to the joint family background were 38 in number constituting 34.86 per cent. It would be pertinent to mention here that those who belonged to joint family background had larger household than those of the nuclear family background and, therefore, it would be somewhat unreasonable to presume that they adhered to the ideal typical norms (residential unity of three generations) of joint family.

So far as the age profile of the panchayat members was concerned, it was somewhat remarkable to note that it ranged between 21 and 65 years. The majority of the panchayat members, however, came from 31 to 50 years of age group constituting 56.87 per cent of the total. The relatively young members were just 18 in number constituting 16.51 per cent. The members belonging the age group 51 and above were 29 in number constituting 26.60 per cent. It is safe to conclude here

Table 4.3

Social profile of the Panchas in the Dalit-headed villages: Kalanaur

Population	*Anwal*	*Lahli*	*Patwa-pur*	*Niga-na*	*Kah-naur*	*Temur-pur*	*Total*
Family type and village							
Nuclear family	11	7	5	5	15	6	49
Joint/Extended family	-	1	2	9	-	2	14
Age groups							
21-30 yrs.	2	2	2	1	4	2	13
31-40 yrs.	2	2	2	2	5	2	15
41-50 yrs.	5	4	2	3	4	2	20
51 and above	2	-	1	8	2	2	15
Education and village							
Illiterate	3	4	2	6	5	3	23
Middle and upper middle	3	4	4	7	7	4	29
Secondary and Senior secondary	2	-	1	1	1	1	6
Graduate and above	3	-	-	-	2	-	5
Income and village							
0-2500	7	4	4	9	8	6	38
2501-3500	-	1	1	3	2	1	8
3501-4500	-	-	1	-	-	-	1
4501-5500	2	2	1	1	5	-	11
5501-6500	-	-	-	-	-	1	1
6501 and above	2	1	-	1	-	-	4
Caste category and village							
Upper caste	5	3	1	1	8	4	22
Middle caste	-	1	-	1	2	1	5
Lower caste	6	4	6	12	5	3	36
Occupation and village							
Agriculture	6	3	-	4	4	2	19
Agricultural labourer	2	5	5	8	9	6	35
Service and others	3	-	2	2	2	-	9
Sex and village							
Male	6	4	4	10	11	6	41
Female	5	4	3	4	4	2	22

Table 4.4

Social profile of the Panchas in the non-Dalit-headed villages: Kalanaur

Population	*Sanga-hera*	*Jind-ran*	*Gud-han*	*Masud-pur*	*Kher-adi*	*Mada-udi Radhi-yan*	*Total*	*Grand Total*
Family type and village								
Nuclear family	3	5	5	4	2	3	22	71 (65.13)
Joint/Extended family	3	2	6	2	8	3	24	38 (34.86)
Age groups								
21-30 yrs.	1	1	1	-	-	2	5	18 (18.51)
31-40 yrs.	2	2	3	3	3	1	14	29 (26.60)
41-50 yrs.	1	3	2	2	3	2	13	33 (30.27)
51 and above	2	1	5	1	4	1	14	29 (26.60)
Education and village								
Illiterate	4	2	4	1	3	1	15	38 (34.86)
Middle and upper middle	1	5	6	5	4	4	25	54 (49.54)
Secondary and Sr. secondary	-	-	1	-	2	1	4	10 (9.17)
Graduate and above	1	-	-	-	1	-	2	7 (6.42)
Income and village								
0-2500	2	3	4	1	7	1	18	56 (51.37)
2501-3500	-	1	4	-	2	3	10	18 (16.51)
3501-4500	1	-	-	1	-	-	2	3 (2.75)
4501-5500	3	2	-	3	1	2	11	22 (20.18)
5501-6500	-	1	-	-	-	-	1	2 (1.83)
6501 and above	-	-	3	1	-	-	4	8 (7.33)
Caste category and village								
Upper caste	3	3	6	4	2	1	19	41 (37.61)
Middle caste	1	3	1	1	1	2	9	14 (12.84)
Lower caste	2	1	4	1	7	3	18	54 (49.54)
Occupation and village								
Agriculture	3	2	5	4	5	2	21	40 (36.69)
Agricultural labourer	3	4	6	2	4	4	23	58 (53.21)
Service and others	-	1	-	-	1	-	2	11 (10.09)
Sex and village								
Male	3	4	9	4	7	5	32	73 (66.97)
Female	3	3	2	2	3	1	14	36 (33.02)

Note: Figures in parenthesis show percentage.

that the members' age profile reveals that the relatively young members are represented as Panchas. The elderly members as such do not take active interest in participating actively in local body.

Regarding the educational background of the respondents, it was noticed that majority of the panchayat members were either illiterate or had education up to the middle level. Out of 109 members, 38 (34.86%) were illiterate, 54 (49.54%) were educated upto the upper middle level, 10 (9.17%) upto the senior secondary level and only 7 (6.42%) were graduate. This gives us an idea that the education profile of the panchayat members does not suggest any increase in the level of education.

So far as the income background of the Panchas is concerned, majority of them had their income ranging between Rs. 0-3,500 per month. The income background of the members reveals that 67.88 per cent of them had their income not above Rs. 3,500. The members who earned more than Rs. 6,501 per month were restricted to 8 (7.33%) only. It is also interesting to mention here that majority of the members, i.e., 98 out of 109 i.e. nearly 90 per cent had their primary source of earning from agriculture only. Either they were agricultural labourer or had a little land as the major source of their livelihood.

The findings of the present study reveal that gender and caste barriers still pose a major impediment before the leaders. The leaders representing women and SC groups have not yet been in a position to carry along with them the trust of people so as to transcend the barriers of gender and caste and the traditional mindset. On the contrary, at some places, the government's affirmative measures to uplift Dalits have become the flashpoint of caste hostility resulting into caste violence. The members of Dalit community have similarly been targeted and have suffered many atrocities without adequate protection and redressal of their grievances by the state.

Panchayat Leadership Perception on Caste and Untouchability

In order to ascertain the Panchas' views on social issues, especially related to the problems of removing caste as narrow and sectarian outlook obstructing the life of the village people, certain topics were identified. It was presumed that education could act as an antidote to caste. Similarly, the provision of legal measures against any social injustice, creation of social awareness and education would go a long way in removing the rigid caste attitude. In the studied villages of Dalit-headed

Table 4.5

Population structure and the social characteristics of the Dalit-headed villages: Kalanaur

Population	*Anwal*	*Lahli*	*Patwapur*	*Nigana*	*Kahnaur*	*Temurpur*	*Total*
Total	4312	3334	1606	4886	7611	420	22169
Male	2312 (53.61)	1788 (52.72)	854 (53.17)	2650 (54.23)	4087 (53.69)	228 (54.28)	11919 (54.28)
Female	2000 (46.38)	1546 (46.37)	752 (46.82)	2236 (45.76)	3524 (46.30)	192 (45.71)	10250 (45.71)
0-6 age group							
Total	760	590	279	929	1474	83	4115
Male	397	291	135	479	887	58	2247
Female	363	299	144	450	587	25	1868
SC population							
Total	1504 (34.87)	1232 (36.95)	718 (44.70)	1746 (35.73)	2579 (33.76)	86 (20.47)	7865
Male	808 (18.73)	674 (20.21)	385 (23.97)	979 (20.03)	1398 (18.36)	28 (6.66)	4272
Female	696 (16.14)	558 (16.73)	333 (20.73)	767 (15.69)	1172 (15.39)	58 (13.80)	3584
Literacy							
Total	2337 (54.19)	1657 (49.70)	775 (48.25)	1747 (33.75)	3946 (51.84)	231 (55.10)	1693
Male	1480 (34.32)	1141 (34.22)	515 (32..06)	1691 (34.60)	2613 (34.33)	135 (32.14)	7575
Female	857 (19.87)	516 (15.47)	260 (16.18)	56 (1.14)	1333 (17.51)	96 (22.85)	3118

Note: Figures in parenthesis show percentage.

Sarpanch, it was found that the majority, i.e., 47 out of 63 (74.60%) members, felt that by promoting education, the caste-minded behaviour could be restrained, but 16 (25.39%) members did not feel so. On the contrary, it was found that 25.39 per cent people still vote on caste lines (see Tables 4.8 and 4.9).

Table 4.6

Population structure and the social characteristics of the non-Dalit-headed villages: Kalanaur

Population	*Sangahera*	*Jindran*	*Gudhan*	*Masudpur*	*Kheradi*	*Madaudi Radhyan*	*Total*	*Grand Total*
Total	1737	1698	3358	1022	2293	1387	11495	33664
Male	922 (53.08)	911 (53.65)	1819 (54.16)	552 (54.01)	1242 (54.16)	762 (54.93)	6208	18127
Female	815 (46.91)	787 (46.34)	1539 (45.83)	470 (45.98)	1051 (45.83)	625 (45.06)	5287	15537
0-6 age group								
Total	357	335	533	178	378	265	2046	6161
Male	192	171	296	96	192	151	1098	3345
Female	165	164	237	82	186	114	948	2816
SC population								
Total	332 (19.11)	270 (15.90)	516 (15.36)	80 (7.82)	1251 (54.55)	570 (41.09)	3019	10884
Male	184 (10.59)	142 (8.36)	274 (8.15)	49 (4.79)	670 (29.21)	311 (22.42)	1630	5902
Female	148 (8.52)	128 (7.53)	242 (7.20)	31 (3.03)	581 (25.33)	259 (18.67)	1389	4973
Literacy								
Total	781 (44.96)	735 (43.28)	1306 (38.89)	531 (51.95)	1092 (47.62)	649 (46.79)	5094	15787
Male	560 (32.23)	526 (31.09)	957 (28.49)	368 (36.00)	767 (33.44)	439 (31.65)	3617	11192
Female	221 (12.72)	209 (12.30)	349 (10.39)	163 (15.94)	325 (14.17)	210 (15.14)	1477	4595

Note: Figures in parenthesis show percentage.

Table 4.7

Population, literacy and sex ratio in Haryana (Meham and Rohtak)

State/Dist./Tehsil	*Persons*	*Male*	*Female*	*Sex Ratio*	*Sex Ratio (0-6)*
Haryana					
Total (Haryana)	21082989	11327658	9755331	861	820
Rural	14968850	8017622	6951228	867	824
Urban	6114139	3310036	2804103	847	809
Rohtak District (Total)	940036	508885	431151	847	796
Rural	610486	331899	278587	839	802
Urban	329550	176986	152564	862	781
Meham Tehsil (Total)	181326	98471	82855	841	794
Rural	163160	88729	74431	839	796
Urban	18166	9742	8424	865	775
Rohtak Tehsil (Total)	758710	410414	348296	849	796
Rural	447326	243170	204156	840	805
Urban	311384	167244	144140	862	781
Literacy Haryana	68.59	79.25	56.31		
Rural	63.82	76.13	49.77		
Urban	79.89	86.58	72.05		
Rohtak	74.56	84.29	63.19		
Rural	70.28	82.11	56.29		
Urban	82.26	88.27	75.39		
Meham Tehsil	68.17	80.11	54.14		
Rural	67.11	79.46	52.53		
Urban	77.62	85.92	68.15		
Rohtak Tehsil	70.06	85.28	65.32		
Rural	71.42	83.07	57.65		
Urban	82.53	88.40	75.80		

Table 4.8

Panchas' perception about factors removing caste barriers in Dalit-headed village: Kalanaur

Factors affecting caste feeling	Anwal		Lahli		Patwa-pur		Nigana		Kahn-aur		Temur-pur		Total	
	Y	N	Y	N	Y	N	Y	N	Y	N	Y	N	Y	N
Promotion of education	8	3	6	2	6	1	10	4	11	4	6	2	47	16
Vote on caste line	7	4	6	2	6	1	12	2	11	4	5	3	47	16
Social justice	9	2	6	2	5	2	11	3	12	3	6	2	49	14
Social awareness	8	3	7	1	5	2	9	6	12	3	6	2	49	14
Reservation in job and education	10	1	8	...	7	...	14	...	14	1	8	...	61	2
Total	63													

Table 4.9

Panchas' perception about factors removing caste barriers in non-Dalit-headed villages: Kalanaur

Factors affecting caste feeling	Sanga-hera		Jind-ran		Gud-han		Masud-pur		Kheradi		Madaudi Radhyan		Total		Grand Total	
	Y	N	Y	N	Y	N	Y	N	Y	N	Y	N	Y	N	Y	N
Promotion of education	4	2	5	2	8	3	4	2	7	3	4	2	32	14	79	30
Vote on caste line	4	2	5	2	8	3	4	2	7	3	4	2	32	14	79	30
Social justice	5	1	6	1	9	2	5	1	8	2	5	1	38	08	87	22
Social awareness	5	1	6	1	9	2	5	1	8	2	5	1	38	08	87	22
Reservation in job and education	6	...	7	...	10	1	6	...	10	...	6	...	45	01	106	03

There was strong perception in the mind of Panchas that social justice and social awareness need to be taken up seriously in case the rigid caste feeling has to be removed. On both these issues, 49 out of 63 Panchas (77.77%) felt that people were disillusioned with state apparatus in granting justice to the SCs being victims of caste prejudices, who face discrimination and atrocities. And, therefore, they believed that it was on this issue that a programme of social awareness campaign could be successful in launching a crusade against the act of social injustice. Nevertheless, 14 (22.20%) of Panchas were not very optimistic about it as they felt that on matters relating to the question of granting justice, there is a traditional and feudal mind which works and makes it difficult to eradicate caste feeling. Almost all the Panchas, i.e., 106 out of 109 (97.24%), excepting 3 (2.75%), held that the reservation in job and education should continue for the Dalits.

It was interesting to note that both in Dalit-headed and non-Dalit-headed villages, it was perceived that reservation has been a major factor in empowering Dalits economically and politically. And, there is a general perception that both these factors, i.e., economic and political upliftment, are instrumental in transcending caste barrier. In Dalit-headed villages, 61 out of 63 (96.82%) Panchas felt that reservation was a critical factor in removing caste barriers, whereas in non-Dalit-headed villages 45 out of 46 (97.82%) Panchas considered it to be a crucial factor.

Functioning of Panchayat Leadership

It was also found that there were many factors which might make Dalit leadership effective. Some of the issues relating to this aspect corresponded with many factors but here only those responses were collected which were found useful. The responses were collected on eight factors, namely, reservation in politics, women's reservation in politics, construction of separate *chaupals* for Dalits, legal remedies to check atrocities on Dalits, separate political party of Dalits, separate polling booth for Dalits, Dalits representation in higher positions in government offices and a separate political party of the Dalits (see Tables 4.10 and 4.11).

Table 4.10

Panchas' perception about factors making Dalit leaders politically effective in Dalit-headed villages: Kalanaur

Factors affecting political upliftment	*Anwal*		*Lahli*		*Patwa-pur*		*Nigana*		*Kahn-aur*		*Temur-pur*		*Total*	
	Y	*N*	*Y*	*N*	*Y*	*N*	*Y*	*N*	*Y*	*N*	*Y*	*N*	*Y*	*N*
Reservation in politics	7	4	6	2	5	2	8	6	11	4	5	3	42	21
Women reservation in politics	6	5	5	3	4	3	7	7	7	8	5	3	34	29
Separate chapels for Dalits	5	6	5	3	4	3	6	8	12	3	4	4	41	22
Legal remedies to check atrocities	7	4	5	3	5	2	9	5	12	3	6	2	44	19
Separate party for Dalits	7	4	5	3	5	2	9	5	12	3	6	2	44	19
Separate polling booths	5	6	4	4	4	3	6	8	8	7	4	4	30	33
Representation in government office	7	4	6	2	5	2	10	4	12	3	6	2	46	17
Political organization	7	4	5	3	5	2	10	4	12	3	6	2	45	18

On the question of reservation in politics, 75 out of 106 Panchas (68.80%) felt that it was essential because without their politically occupying positions at the local level, they could not be effective. Similarly, they held the opinion that women's reservation in politics would also ensure their representation in politics, but the enthusiasm was not all that encouraging because out of 109, only 65 (59.63%) deemed it to be a positive step, whereas 44 (40.36%) felt that women leadership has its

Table 4.11

Panchas perception about factors making Dalit leaders politically effective in non-Dalit-headed villages: Kalanaur

Factors affecting political upliftment	*Sanga-hera*		*Jindran*		*Gud-han*		*Masud-pur*		*Kheradi*		*Madaudi*		*Total*		*Grand*	
	Y	*N*	*Y*	*N*	*Y*	*N*	*Y*	*N*	*Y*	*N*	*Y*	*N*	*Y*	*N*	*Y*	*N*
Reservation in politics	5	1	5	2	8	3	4	2	7	3	4	2	33	13	75	34
Women reservation in politics	4	2	5	2	7	4	4	2	7	3	4	2	31	15	65	44
Separate chapels for Dalits	4	2	4	3	6	5	3	3	5	5	3	3	25	21	66	43
Legal remedies to check atrocities	5	1	5	2	9	2	5	1	8	2	4	2	36	10	77	32
Separate party for Dalits	5	1	5	2	8	3	4	2	7	3	3	3	32	14	76	33
Separate polling booths	3	3	3	4	6	5	3	3	6	4	3	3	24	22	54	55
Representation in government office	5	1	6	1	9	2	5	1	8	2	4	2	37	09	83	26
Political organization	5	1	5	2	8	3	4	2	8	2	4	2	34	12	79	30

own limitations. Very often, they play a surrogate role to their male counterparts who appropriate their power and become *de facto* leaders. Separate *chaupal* was not a major issue because they stated that the SC people in the block already hold their meetings in their own *chaupal*. But still 66 (60.55%) Panchas felt it to be important while 43 out of 106 (39.44%) considered it not a very important factor. For 77 Panchas (70.64%) legal measures to check atrocities on Dalits were an important step which could make the leadership quite effective, but 32 out of 106 (29.35%) did not feel so. Out of 109, 76 Panchas, i.e., (69.72%) believed that a separate political party for the SCs could make them effective, while 33 (30.27%) felt otherwise. As regards representation in government offices, 83 (76.14%) considered it crucial while 26 (23.85%) did not feel so. And, 70 out of 109 (72.47%) felt political organization to be quite effective, while 30 (27.52%) did not find it to be effective.

It was also interesting to find that on certain issues even the Dalits admitted that they are better off in comparison to their fellow castemen, who still suffer from powerlessness and appalling poverty. On the issue of Dalits having separate polling booths at the time of elections, 65 (50.15%) Panchas did not consider it to be an important step as they stated that Dalits are allowed to cast vote as they have never been obstructed by anyone in exercising their right to vote. On matters concerning representation of Dalits in higher positions of government offices, 83 Panchas (76.14%) felt that adequate representation could be extremely beneficial. They found that the persons on higher positions in government belonging to upper caste tended to show discrimination by not helping them out and, therefore, they felt that their own members on these positions could be quite crucial. Still 26 (23.85%) Panchas did not consider it to be a very important factor. Out of 109, 79 (72.47%) Panchas felt that a separate political party, exclusively of Dalits, could go a long way in improving the functioning of Dalit leaders. They had in mind the formation of Bahujan Samaj Party founded by Kanshi Ram in 1984, which has supported Mayawati to become the Chief Minister of Uttar Pradesh on two occasions.

Factors Posing Problems in Effective Functioning of Dalit Leaders

As regards the traditional mindsets posing problems for effective functioning of Dalit leadership, five factors, mainly relating to culture and tradition, were identified. They were: (a) entry into temple, (b) conversion, (c) self-dignity, (d) social taboos regarding inter-dining restrictions, and (e) socio-cultural organization of the Dalits (see Tables 4.12 and 4.13).

Table 4.12

Panchas' perception about factors posing problems for Dalit leaders in Dalit-headed villages: Kalanaur

Factors affecting traditional mindsets	*Anwal*		*Lahli*		*Patwa-pur*		*Nigana*		*Kahn-aur*		*Temur-pur*		*Total*	
	Y	*N*	*Y*	*N*	*Y*	*N*	*Y*	*N*	*Y*	*N*	*Y*	*N*	*Y*	*N*
Entry of Dalits in temple	8	3	5	3	5	2	10	4	11	4	5	3	44	19
Dalits conversion	8	3	6	2	5	2	11	3	11	4	6	2	47	16
Dalit's self-dignity	6	5	5	3	4	3	8	6	10	5	5	3	38	25
Social taboos	6	5	4	4	4	3	9	5	8	7	5	3	36	27
Socio-cultural organization	7	4	5	3	5	2	9	5	10	5	6	2	41	21

Table 4.13

Panchas perception about factors posing problems for Dalit leaders in non-Dalit-headed villages: Kalanaur

Factors affecting traditional mindsets	*Sanga-hera*		*Jindran*		*Gud-han*		*Masud-pur*		*Kheradi*		*Madaudi Radhyan*		*Total*		*Grand Total*	
	Y	*N*	*Y*	*N*	*Y*	*N*	*Y*	*N*	*Y*	*N*	*Y*	*N*	*Y*	*N*	*Y*	*N*
Entry of Dalits in temple	4	2	5	1	8	3	4	2	7	3	4	2	32	13	76	32
Dalits conversion	4	2	5	1	8	3	4	2	7	3	4	2	32	14	79	29
Dalit's self-dignity	4	2	4	2	7	4	3	3	5	5	3	3	26	19	64	44
Social taboos	3	3	3	4	6	5	3	3	4	6	3	3	22	24	58	51
Socio-cultural organization	3	3	4	3	7	4	4	2	7	3	4	2	29	17	70	28

The Panchas accorded greater importance to the discrimination shown towards them. Out of 109, 76 (69.72%) felt that not allowing the members of the SCs to enter temple had created major obstacle in removing caste barriers. In reaction to atrocities, members of the SCs felt very depressed and that was the reason why they were forced to go for conversion as a desperate measure to express their anguish. Out of 109, 79 (72.47%) Panchas were of the opinion that Dalits opting for conversion was in response to the denial of justice to them. In spite of the discrimination and atrocities, 29 (26.60%) held that conversion was no answer to the solution of their problem. Quite a few of them felt that excessive caste discriminatory attitude affected their pride and self-dignity. And, 64 (58.71%) felt that Dalit self-dignity is an important factor. The manner in which they are treated has not shown improvement in their self-dignity. Some of the Dalit Panchas also narrated that social taboos, such as interdining restrictions and implicit notions of untouchability, also posed problems in the effective functioning of Dalit leaders. About 85 (77.98%) felt that the formation of a socio-cultural organization could help Dalits to create their own reference group, which would help them restore their self-dignity and pride.

Leadership and its Functioning in Removing Gender Barrier

Raj Bala, Sarpanch belonging to Chamar caste in Anwal village, was of the opinion that she was already hard pressed with her drudgery of homework and on top of it, she has to take care of the additional burden of panchayat work for which she hardly considered herself fit. She also pointed out that she has a grown up daughter to be married and if she is required to go to block office for panchayat work, her mind always remained preoccupied with household work. She was hardly inclined to contest election for the second term. Her lamentation was that sooner she gets rid of the panchayat work, better it would be for her. She had a distinct perception of leadership. She felt that the leadership is something which is a male exclusive job as they have nothing better to do besides it suits their temperament as well.

But, the experience of Chand Tari, the Sarpanch of Patwapur was not as disheartening. She was quite happy with the kind of status that she gained after becoming Sarpanch. All her work related to office was being handled by her son Rajinder, who is B.A., B. Ed. and has his own tailoring shop. Since her mother was elected in a keenly contested election for the post of Panch, therefore, the enthusiasm and jubilation was conspicuously noticed both on Rajinder's and his mother's face. Chand Tari feels let down by others because she felt that the division existing on the caste line is so strong that whenever the meeting is convened all the Panchas do not turn up. But she stated that she has got some dependable panchayat members from within her own caste and, therefore, she does not feel isolated. The panchayat members of Chamar caste give her full cooperation in panchayat work. Just in case, she is required to go to block office, she takes them along. But she felt that in the offices, the behaviour of the menfolks and the office people is not positive. They have a tendency to be casual and, therefore, she relies more on her son for the office work. Her son also shared this information with a sense of pride that all office matters are looked after by him and he is instrumental in getting his mother's signature appended.

So far as the non-Dalit-headed villages were concerned, next to Gudhan village, Kheradi had 2,293 population and Sangahera and Jindran ranked below it with 1,737 and 1,698 population respectively. Masudpur was the smallest village among the studied villages with a population of 1,022. In all these villages, the deficit of female was between 7 to 10 per 100 males, which is well above the state average and borders close to the Kalanaur block's average figure of 883.

It is pertinent to mention here that the statistics of population given in Table 4.6 clearly show that Kheradi has the largest concentration of the SC population. No wonder, it has a Sarpanch, a young enthusiast belonging to Dhanak caste.

Madaudi Radhiyan is also a small village having a population of 1,387. And this village also has majority of people belonging to SCs. Its SC population consists of 41.09 per cent of the total. Except these two villages, namely, Kheradi and Madaudi Radhiyan, in all other studied non-Dalit-headed villages, the concentration of SCs was below the state average. In descending order, it was recorded in Sangahera (19.11%) Jindran (15.90%), Gudhan (15.36%) and lowest in Masudpur (7.28%). The gap in literacy percentage between male and female was also quite striking (see Table 4.6). It ranged between 15 and 20. The average male literacy in the non-Dalit-headed villages was reported to be 32.28, whereas the average for the female literacy was 13.44. That means the gap in literacy between male and female was 18.84.

Dalit Leaders Dovetail the Politics of High-Caste People

One of the reasons why the Dalit leaders are not very effective at the panchayat level is that they very often play a surrogate role in high-caste politics. In other words, they carry the burden of high-caste politics on their shoulders, which creates division within their own rank and makes them all the more vulnerable. In order to inquire about the factors responsible for it, following factors were identified and the responses on them were categorically ascertained from the Panchas. The factors pertained to: (a) vested interest, (b) lack of education, (c) political compulsion, (d) lack of their own leaders, and (e) lack of self-confidence (see Tables 4.14 and 4.15).

When inquired about the Panchas' perception on vested interest as the factor responsible for Dalit leaders playing into the hands of high-caste people, out of 109, 81 (74.31%) felt that it was the vested interest of the Dalit leaders which made them follow the politics of high-caste people, while 28 (25.68%) did not consider it to be an important factor. About 80 (73.39%) of the Panchas' perception was that it was the lack of education which made them pursue high-caste politics, but 29 (26.60%) of them did not consider it an important factor. Some of the

Table 4.14

Panchas' perception about factors forcing Dalit leaders to do politics of high-caste people in Dalit-headed villages: Kalanaur

Factors affecting high caste people	Anwal		Lahli		Patwa-pur		Nigana		Kahnaur		Temur-pur		Total	
	Y	N	Y	N	Y	N	Y	N	Y	N	Y	N	Y	N
Vested interest	9	2	5	3	5	2	11	3	2	3	6	2	48	15
Lack of education	8	3	6	2	5	2	10	4	11	4	6	2	46	17
Political compulsion	7	4	6	2	5	2	10	4	11	4	5	3	44	19
Lack of Dalit leaders	7	4	6	2	6	1	11	3	11	4	5	3	46	17
Lack of self-confidence	8	3	6	2	6	1	11	3	12	3	6	2	49	14

Table 4.15

Panchas' perception about factors forcing Dalit leaders to do politics of high-caste people in non-Dalit-headed villages: Kalanaur

Factors affecting high caste people	Sanga-hera		Jindran		Gud-han		Masud-pur		Kheradi		Mada-udi		Total		Grand Total	
	Y	N	Y	N	Y	N	Y	N	Y	N	Y	N	Y	N	Y	N
Vested interest	4	2	5	2	8	3	4	2	8	2	4	2	33	13	81	28
Lack of education	5	1	5	2	8	3	5	1	7	3	4	2	34	12	80	29
Political compulsion	5	1	5	2	7	4	5	1	7	3	3	3	32	14	76	33
Lack of Dalit leaders	4	2	4	3	8	3	4	2	6	4	4	2	30	16	76	33
Lack of self-confidence	5	1	5	2	9	2	5	1	8	2	4	2	36	10	85	24

Panchas felt that for the Dalit leaders, it was a *fait accompli* to toe the line of high-caste politics because they derive their own existence from the political party, with which they had an affiliation. Besides, they did not have their own leader belonging to their caste and community who could guide them in an exclusive manner. Seventy-six, out of 109 (69.72%) of the Panchas, were of the opinion that it was the political compulsion and the absence of their own leaders, which made them fall in line with the politics of high-caste people, whereas, 33 (30.27%) of Panchas did not consider it to be an important factor. There were still a large number of Panchas, i.e., 76 (69.72%) who attributed absence of Dalit leaders responsible for playing proxy to high caste people's wishes. There were 85 Panchas (77.98%), who felt it was due to the lack of self-confidence that they agreed to do so. Only 29 Panchas (22%) did not consider this to be an important factor.

In the studied villages from the Kalanaur block, especially where Dalit-headed panchayats existed, i.e., in Anwal, Lahli, Patwapur, Nigana, Kahanaur and Temurpur, the concentration of SC population was 35 per cent. The domination of so-called AJGAR (Ahir, Jat, Gujjar, Rajput) group was not the characteristic feature in these villages. The refugee Punjabis were made to settle in some of these villages, who did not believe in maintaining the rigid scruples of caste-minded discriminatory practices. In spite of all this, it was the absence of education and prosperity that reminded the SCs of their precarious existence in the social, economic and political fields. Even in the studied villages of non-Dalit-headed Sarpanch, i.e., Sangahera, Jindran, Gudhan, Masudpur, Kheradi and Madaudi Radhyan, the mean average of SCs population was about 25 per cent. Kheradi and Madaudi Radhiyan had SCs population constituting 54.55 per cent and 41.09 per cent respectively. The overall situation that obtained in all these villages with regard to the treatment of Dalits was to forge harmonious relations of co-existence, whereby the idea was not to deny the Dalit leaders their due share in their social, economic and political upliftment. Therefore, the opinion expressed by the Panchas was largely related to their independent political status and identity. They felt that the Dalit leaders had yet not been in a position to carve out an independent political space for assuming a distinct role in Haryana's state politics as is the case elsewhere, i.e., in Uttar Pradesh, Maharashtra and some of the southern states.

Factors Improving Dalit Leaders Functioning

In course of the present study, an attempt was made to collect information with the help of interview schedule from all the elected members of the gram panchayat. Out of 127, information was collected from 109 Panchas, which included 73 (66.97%) male Panchas and 36 (33.02%) female Panchas. What problems they encountered in working with the people, how they could overcome the caste barrier, how they could be effective in working with the people and what factors they perceived were important to fall in line with the upper-caste politics and why there exist internal divisions within them – were some of the issues, which were the main focus of the present study. Finally, in the present study, an attempt was also made to ascertain as to what perception they had about making the Dalit leadership all the more effective. On the basis of their views, seven factors were found to be useful and therefore our investigation centred around those factors. It was also presumed that some of the factors could be useful for the effective functioning of Dalit leaders at the village level. The factors were: (a) economic independence, (b) removal of atrocity, (c) political participation of the Dalits, (d) granting social justice to Dalits, (e) promoting education among them, (f) continuation of reservation policy for the SCs, and (g) no change in the present reservation policy (see Tables 4.16 and 4.17).

Table 4.16

Panchas' perception about factors improving Dalit's leaders functioning in Dalit-headed villages: Kalanaur

Factors improving Dalit's leadership	*Anwal*		*Lahli*		*Patwa-pur*		*Nigana*		*Kahn-aur*		*Temur-pur*		*Total*	
	Y	*N*	*Y*	*N*	*Y*	*N*	*Y*	*N*	*Y*	*N*	*Y*	*N*	*Y*	*N*
Economic independence	7	4	5	3	5	2	9	5	11	4	5	3	42	29
Removal of atrocity	8	3	6	2	6	1	10	4	12	3	5	3	47	16
Political participation	7	4	5	3	5	2	8	6	10	5	4	4	39	24
Social justice	9	2	6	2	6	1	10	4	12	3	7	1	50	13
Education	7	4	5	3	5	2	10	4	10	5	6	2	43	20
Continuation of reservation	11	...	8	...	7	...	14	...	15	...	8	...	63	...
No change in reservation policy	11	...	8	...	7	...	14	...	15	...	8	...	63	...

Table 4.17

Panchas' perception about factors improving Dalit's leaders functioning in non-Dalit-headed villages: Kalanaur

Factors improving Dalit's leadership	*Sanga-hera*		*Jindran*		*Gud-han*		*Masud-pur*		*Kheradi*		*Madaudi*		*Total*		*G Total*	
	Y	*N*	*Y*	*N*	*Y*	*N*	*Y*	*N*	*Y*	*N*	*Y*	*N*	*Y*	*N*	*Y*	*N*
Economic independence	4	2	5	2	8	3	4	2	8	2	4	2	33	13	75	34
Removal of atrocity	5	1	5	2	9	2	5	1	8	2	5	1	37	09	84	25
Political participation	3	3	4	3	7	4	3	3	7	3	4	2	28	18	67	42
Social justice	5	1	5	2	8	3	4	2	8	2	5	1	35	11	85	24
Education	5	1	5	2	7	4	4	2	7	3	5	1	33	13	76	33
Continuation of reservation	6	...	7	...	11	...	6	...	10	...	6	...	46	...	109	...
No change in reservation policy	6	...	7	...	11	...	6	...	10	...	6	...	46	...	109	...

The findings of the study suggest that 79 out of 109 Panchas (68.80%) believed that economic independence would make the life of Dalit people more focused. The remaining 34 (31.19%) felt it important but did not consider it the most important factor. Majority of the Panchas i.e., 84 (77.06%) considered removal of atrocity as one of the most important activities in case relief is to be provided to the members belonging to the Dalit section. However, 22.93 per cent Panchas did not consider it a very important. Even on the issue of political participation, 67 out 109 Panchas (61.46%) felt it to be the most important factor in solving their problems. But 42 respondents (38.53%) did not feel it so. On the matters related to social justice 85 Panchas out of 109 (77.98%) expressed their strong opinion as they felt it to be important in removing the suffering of the SC people. However, 24 (22.01%) either did not understand its importance or decided to keep quiet by simply saying that they did not consider it very important. On the question of spreading education among them, majority, i.e., 76 (69.22%) had positive attitude as they felt it important, but 33 (30.27%) did not consider it a significant step in improving the lot of the Dalit.

What was surprising to note was a strong attitude and perception of the Panchas of all sections to consider continuation of reservation policy for the upliftment and welfare of the SC people. They felt that it was the reservation policy of the government, which has singularly been helpful in improving the lot of the SC people. They did not consider legal measures such as granting social justice as an important factor for the alleviation of the sufferings of Dalits. However, the non-Dalit Panchas did not fail to mention that there was a need to extend reservation to other communities as well for their improvement. This is an evidence of the fact that the Dalit leaders considered that the only silver lining in improving the lot of Dalits has been the government's reservation policy and they do not want to loose it at any cost.

Summing up

In Haryana, a set of young leaders has emerged within the panchayats both among the Dalits and the non-Dalits even if elected elderly members do not take much interest in participating actively in the local body. However, the study shows that the younger members – particularly Dalits – are handicapped by the fact that a majority of the respondents selected in the study are educated only up to the middle school level and at least one-third are illiterate. This is in keeping with the literacy levels in Haryana. Despite the state being fairly prosperous, the income of a majority of the Panchas is not above Rs 3,500 per month.

One result of this socio-economic backwardness is the continued prevalence of caste-based discrimination and Dalits being the victims of vested interests, prejudice and at times atrocities. Dalit leaders are very disillusioned with the state apparatus, which they feel makes no effort to provide social justice to them. Consequently, they suffer from lack of confidence, political compulsions and lack of strong Dalit leaders both at the local and state levels. Many Dalit leaders felt they should form a socio-cultural organization to mobilize their community. Another option they put forward to deal with untouchability and social distance was conversion, as they are not allowed entry into the local temples. They also felt that education and economic independence from the upper castes would help them improve their status. The present status of Dalits in the state has rendered it difficult for them to function effectively within the panchayats. Women elected to the panchayats do not get a chance in the prevailing patriarchal and feudal set-up to participate at all.

Thus, Haryana provides us an example of a state where the existing caste structure is a major obstacle to the inclusion and the participation of Dalits in the new panchayats. It shows that provision of reservations by itself cannot introduce change in such a social system. Yet, many of the Dalit and non-Dalit leaders in the panchayats feel that reservation should continue as it has provided an avenue of representation and underlined the need for change in the prevailing social structure to the Dalits. Together with reservation, provision of education and support against an oppressive social structure would help in making it worthwhile. The latter would require political will, which the government has not demonstrated so far. An effective leadership from within both the Dalit and non-Dalit-headed panchayats is still in a formative stage and that is why there is a need to remove structural impediments which would help in breaking the institutional bondage.

6

Dalit Leadership in the New Panchayats

A Comparative Analysis

This study has examined the role played by the emerging Dalit leadership in the new panchayats in four selected states. It is now possible to discuss in a comparative vein, the extent to which reservation in the new panchayats has been able to introduce effective representation, inclusion and participation for Dalits leading to democratization of panchayats as structures of local governance. Have Dalits been able to overcome the control that the upper castes/classes had developed over local structures of power? Have they been able to help their own community through implementation of welfare programmes? In short, whether reservation has worked as an instrument of socio-political change at the level of the panchayats.

The present study suggests that reservation has enabled Dalits to enter into the panchayats in large numbers in the states. A critical mass has appeared, which has the potential to introduce change. However, effective and meaningful participation by Dalit leaders is determined by the specific social, economic and political context in which the panchayats are embedded. There are major differences among the states studied which show that context matters. Certain socio-economic factors in the selected states have determined the extent to which Dalits have made use of reservation at the local level and introduced change at the grassroots. In this chapter, an attempt is made to identify and discuss the enabling/disabling factors – social and institutional – in the four states, which have helped or hindered Dalits from making effective use of reservation at the local level. The new emerging Dalit leaders face two problems: opposition from the traditional leadership and an obstructionist attitude from the bureaucracy that is not supportive of the needs of the Dalit leadership. The field studies show that social factors such as age, education, economic situation and the presence/absence of social discrimination play a central role in determining the extent to which Dalits are able to participate meaningfully. These factors provide the potential to Dalits to introduce change in the power structure within panchayats. Similarly, institutional factors are also important: the attitude and role played by the local bureaucracy has a determining effect. Where the local bureaucracy is sympathetic and helpful to the new Dalit leadership, much more can be achieved by it; where an obstructionist or unhelpful attitude prevails, this is not possible. Often, the local bureaucracy joins hands with the upper castes of the area making it difficult for Dalit leaders to implement programmes in a fair manner. A second factor is training imparted to the new panchayat members by the government. The present study indicates that training helps overcome inhibitions, instils confidence and increases knowledge about the running of the panchayat and programmes within it.

The study also points to major differences among the selected states. In Himachal Pradesh (HP), Dalits have not only entered the panchayats but in comparison to the other states, also initiated a process of participation in a limited manner. They have been able to secure a place for themselves in the panchayats, which promises a greater role in the future. At the other end is Madhya Pradesh (MP) where the least change has taken place and the entry of Dalits has yet to show any substantial change. Uttar Pradesh (UP) and Haryana in different ways, as discussed below, fall in between. In both the states, however, some change has taken place due to political mobilization in the former and economic development in the latter. The importance of social factors such as age, education, political consciousness and economic independence in enabling Dalits to function in the panchayats is best seen in the case of HP as compared to MP, UP and Haryana. While Dalits in HP are not able to participate fully in decision-making and panchayats are still largely under the control of the upper castes/classes, their position is much better than in the case of the other three states. The state is in a phase of transition from control by the upper castes to greater sharing of power and influence with the Dalits. Reservations have helped in making this social process move faster. As the field study shows non-Dalits agree that Dalits are capable of making their own decisions and there is fairly good cooperation between the two groups in the panchayats. Dalits also feel that they have gained substantial benefits from the panchayats.

These changes are due to the larger social changes, which have taken place in the state. HP has a literacy rate of about 73 per cent, which is much higher than the national average, and the difference between male and female and Dalit and non-Dalit is lower. The field study points to the rise of relatively younger and better-educated Dalit Sarpanchas. Many of them are between the ages of 25 and 44, are graduates and knowledgeable about the panchayat, its powers and functioning. Many of them are also aware of the panchayat programmes and of the 73rd constitutional amendment. They are knowledgeable about housing programmes and employment opportunities and loans provided by the panchayats. This is true of a small section of the Dalit women elected to the panchayats as well. Dalits are also highly conscious of their rights and in recent years have become assertive too. The state has promoted education over the last two decades and this has also helped the weaker sections. Education appears to be an enabling factor for Dalit leaders, including women, aiding them in understanding the importance of participation in local structures.

Second, although Dalits in HP do not own much land and their living conditions are not as good as in the case of non-Dalits and this puts them at a disadvantage vis-à-vis non-Dalit panchayat leaders, their economic position is better than Dalits in UP or MP. This is because HP is a prosperous state and the economic condition of the population including Dalits is much better than in the other North Indian states. Per capita income is much higher, there are no big landowners, all landholdings are small in the state and Dalits have also taken to horticulture that was earlier a preserve of the better-off upper castes/classes. The state has played a role in promoting horticulture and particularly helped the weaker sections through subsidies and other forms of help. This has helped in promoting economic independence among the Dalits that is not seen in the other states examined. Thus, the socio-economic context in which Dalits are placed is important as it enables them to make better use of reservations. However, the study shows that leadership comes from landowning persons among Dalits though the size of the landholding may be very small.

A third factor, which has helped Dalits in HP, is the caste system, which has always been more mild and social change has been faster than in other states. Consequently, except in some remote areas, untouchability is not practised in public life and social distance is not maintained rigidly making it easier for Dalits to function as members of the panchayats. Dalits can enter into the houses of non-Dalits, participate in religious festivals and their children in schools are not made to sit or eat separately. Common property such as cremation grounds, grazing grounds and panchayat bhawans are open to all. This has allowed Dalits to participate in the panchayats more than in many other states where social restrictions are much higher and creating barriers for them. They are regular in attending meetings and do so under their own will and not under pressure or persuasion of others.

In contrast, while reservation has thrown up a set of Dalit younger leaders in MP, they are not educated or economically as independent as in the case of HP. MP is a backward state and the literacy level is low, which is reflected in the fact that there is little difference between the educational attainments of the large majority of Dalit and non-Dalit respondents, but illiteracy is much higher among the former and the number of matriculates and college educated persons is much higher among the latter. The empirical data show that this has put the elected Dalit members at a disadvantage within the panchayats. The large majority of the respondents did not know about the new panchayats or the 73rd constitutional amendment. They had little knowledge about the activities of the panchayats, the electoral process and the rights and duties of members. Some were not even aware of the percentage of reservation provided for Dalits. Non-Dalit respondents, on the whole, were better informed.

Dalit respondents in MP suffer the further disadvantage as most of them do not own land and are landless labourers within the village making them dependent upon the landowning class. Many are in debt to the local moneylender in order to meet medical and other family needs and most are below the poverty line. As MP is a backward state, many of the non-Dalit panchayat members are also poor but there is a small section of non-Dalits, which is well-off and has traditionally played an important role in the village, which puts it in a position to control the new panchayats. Moreover, in contrast to HP, caste-based discrimination and untouchability are still practised in MP, which do not allow the Dalit representatives to function within the panchayats. As a result, the Dalit leaders face a number of problems: they are not free to take decisions in the meetings, are under pressure to support upper caste members who helped them win elections, and are often in debt to the upper caste members. On the other hand, members of their own community, who have helped them to elect, have high expectations from them that they fail to fulfil leading to unhappiness and lack of support. Consequently, only a small section of the Dalit villagers attend the Gram Sabha meetings as they feel they have nothing to gain as some of the specific problems faced by Dalits such as lack of employment opportunities, landlessness, loan facility etc. are not discussed or addressed. Many Dalits feel that the panchayat despite having Dalit members has not done anything to remove untouchability, which they feel is the root of all their problems.

Consequently, while Dalits have entered into the new panchayats, they are not in a position to effectively participate in the decision-making process. As the study shows, many respondents pointed out that nobody listened to them or to their suggestions. Some have even decided not to contest for election again as it does not give them any advantage and cuts into the time they spend in earning their living. Many respondents hence felt that reservation facility is not sufficient to empower Dalits and many other problems faced by them must also be addressed by the government.

UP presents a contrast to the other selected states. Like MP, it is a backward state where Dalits have undergone discrimination and disabling poverty though literacy rates have been rising faster over the last two decades. During the 1980s the economy showed signs of growth improving the conditions of Dalits in parts of the state but the 1990s have experienced a downward trend due to endemic political instability in the state. More important is that the Dalits have experienced since the mid-1980s a strong wave of political mobilization based on Dalit identity by the BSP. However, the study shows that mere mobilization cannot be a means of change in the power structure at the panchayat level. There are marked differences in the socio-economic profile of the Dalit and non-Dalit respondents in the study putting the former at a distinct disadvantage.

The 73rd Constitutional Amendment has brought a younger generation into the panchayats but 30 per cent of them are illiterate and 36 per cent just literate which means that more than half have little educational attainments. While there was considerable enthusiasm in contesting for elections, the ability and understanding of the new leadership of the process of local development remains poor. Most of the Dalits required the support of the upper caste influential members of the village including former Pradhans to win the election. All Dalit respondents agreed that without reservation and the support of the local notables they would not have been able to enter into the panchayats. Few were aware of the latest programmes in the panchayats and require the support of the upper castes and Pradhan to obtain the approval for schemes put forward by them.

Dalits also suffer the disadvantage of landlessness making most of them sharecroppers dependent upon the landowning class in the villages. In contrast, the non-Dalit leaders are older, better educated, economically better off and more capable of managing the affairs of the panchayat. Most of the Dalit respondents agreed that while caste is important, lack of social awareness and non-cooperation from villagers and even leaders opposed to change, particularly the attempt by Dalit women to contest for election is a significant obstacle to their functioning in the panchayats. A second factor is factionalism and jealousy on the part of groups, which formerly held power and try to protect their interests. While political parties play a role in the elections and may help Dalit candidates to win, they do not have a presence in the running of the panchayats. Hence, the rise of the BSP has not helped Dalits in the day-to-day affairs of the panchayats. Faced with these problems, at least 70 per cent of the Dalit respondents felt that education and training was needed to help overcome them. Another problem found in a number of states but clearly seen in UP is divisions among the Dalits along sub-caste lines which prevents organized and planned action on their part. Different groups prefer to support their own interests rather than those of the community as a whole.

Caste-based hierarchy and conservative social structure dependent on land, religion and identity still remain important in the villages in UP and the panchayat is not a democratic structure. While untouchability exists, it is limited to personal relationships such as eating together or visiting each other's houses. However, active discrimination is not practised and when differences of opinion arise in the panchayat between the Dalit and non-Dalit members, the latter do not react openly or take action but do prevent the former from freely voicing their opinion. Their superior social status and educational abilities enable them to do so. The rise of the BSP and rising awareness among Dalits, which leads them to file cases against the non-Dalits in the police station, are important deterrents. Despite this, a number of the Dalit respondents felt that unless measures to improve inter-caste and inter-community relationships were taken, they would not be able to participate in the panchayats. They pointed out that it is not the upper castes but the OBCs who form the major landowning group, with whom their relationships were strained. This relationship enters into the functioning of the panchayats creating strain and often conflict. What is noticed is that the Dalits are attempting to improve their position and gain greater control over the panchayats as they have become more assertive than in MP but the non-Dalits are reluctant to share power with them but do not use open force as in the past. At the same time, a section of the non-Dalits feel that the Dalits need assistance in the form of education and formal training and take the trouble to help them in the panchayat. But, the number of this group is small. However, it shows that relationships are changing due to the necessity of working together and the gradually growing desire to have a better working system at the local level that promotes development for all the villagers. There is as yet little equality of participation but it is growing. The ability of Dalit leaders to develop social skills and self-confidence to deal with such obstacles is as important as the need to gain education. In fact, it can be argued that economic and political reasons allow untouchability and caste-based discrimination to continue and if Dalits are able to overcome these problems reservation in the panchayats could have played an important role.

Haryana is a small but developed state and the condition of Dalits is better here than in UP or MP. It has witnessed growth due to the Green Revolution and the resulting agricultural prosperity has trickled down to the Dalits and improved their lives in many ways. The study shows that as in cases of the other states both the Dalit and non-Dalit respondents were young and enthusiastic participating in the panchayat. The elderly persons do not take much interest in the functioning of the panchayats. Women were also well represented though more among the non-Dalits than the Dalits. However, majority of the Panchas were either illiterate or had received education upto the middle level only with very few graduates compared to the other states. Although, a prosperous state as in the case of HP, literacy levels still remain low. Rohtak is the most literate district so far as Dalits are concerned. Society is largely agrarian and the government has not made much effort until very recently to improve literacy levels. The literacy levels among the Dalits are low but there is considerable difference as our study reveals between male and female Dalit respondents. There is a definite gender bias against girls with very few attending school.

Dalits own little land while most of the land is in the hands of the Jats who form the locally dominant landowning group. Consequently, the income levels of the Dalits are lower and they remain dependent on the landowners for employment. Haryana remains predominantly an agricultural state, few industries have been set up and the number of urban areas to which Dalits can migrate for jobs are few. The upper caste groups of Brahmins, Khatri and Aroras, including their women, are well represented in the panchayats. However, compared to Dalits in UP and MP, due to demand for agricultural labour, Dalits in the state are better off and a smaller proportion is below the poverty line. More important than their economic status, Dalits are affected by the fact that Haryana remains socially backward being a feudal, caste-based and patriarchal society. It has witnessed in recent years numerous caste-based atrocities against Dalits, particularly in areas where they have improved their economic situation, which the Jats feel is a threat to their position in the state. Caste and gender remain barriers before Dalit leaders who have not been able to carry along all sections of the Dalit community leave alone the rest of the population. In some places reservations have become the reason for hostility leading to caste violence. As a result, Dalits have suffered many atrocities without adequate protection and redressal of their grievances. The result is a narrow and sectarian mindset which obstructs change. Most people still vote on caste lines. Dalit leaders in panchayats feel that issues of social justice need to be taken up seriously if rigid caste feelings have to be removed. Programmes of social awareness were required for launching a crusade against caste.

Hence, culture and tradition are the two factors that determine the functioning of the panchayats. These do not allow the Dalits to effectively participate in the panchayats. One of the reasons why Dalits have not succeeded in making a mark in the panchayats is that they often play a supportive role to the upper caste leaders in the village due to political compulsions in order to win in elections. This leads to divisions among the Dalits and makes them more vulnerable and dependent upon the upper castes. The reasons lie in the lack of education and the absence of leadership within the community. In fact, it was felt that Dalits in Haryana had failed to carve out a political space for themselves in the politics of the state as in UP, Maharashtra and southern states.

Despite these problems Dalit respondents feel that reservation has been a major factor in empowering them economically and politically. There is also a strong perception among Dalit leaders that economic and political upliftment is instrumental in transcending the caste barrier. Particularly in

Dalit majority villages it was felt that reservation was a critical factor in helping Dalits gain inclusion and participation in panchayats and it should continue in both education and employment so that Dalits can advance upwards and achieve equal status. It was also felt that reservation could give important high posts to Dalits, which would help in upliftment of the community. However, according to many, creation of social awareness was important in removing caste rigidity. In fact, such factors were given equal importance as education in removing caste barriers. Continuing and in fact increasing reservations for women was held as important for making Dalit leadership effective. Other factors pointed out were political organization and a political party along the lines of the BSP. In fact, the Dalit leaders felt that they were better off than their community brethren in other states who were still steeped in appalling poverty and had little employment. Dalit leaders argued that removal of social taboos on inter-dining, socio-cultural organizations of Dalits, building of self-dignity and confidence were the factors that could help. If not conversion was seen as the road to take. Thus, in Haryana, there is a strong feeling among Dalit leaders that politics is the means by which the upliftment of Dalits can take place and they gave it more importance than education.

Apart from the social factors, institutional factors were also important in all the states under study in determining the role played by Dalits in the new panchayats. As villagers view the panchayat as a 'sarkari' organization through which they receive help in improving the village, their relationship with the local bureaucracy is of crucial importance. There were differences in the manner in which the Dalit leadership interacted with the local bureaucracy, which affect their ability to participate and obtain benefits from the panchayats. In HP the relationship between the members of the panchayats including the Dalit Panchas is good and there is a perception that maintaining that relationship is important for the welfare of the village. Funds are received from the bureaucracy and development activities are organized by them. Poor relationship would mean delay in getting funds and delay in execution of programmes. Respondents also pointed out that training programmes are also organized from time to time for Pradhans and Up-Pradhans and ward members at both block and district levels to help them administer the panchayats and in financial management. They felt that such programmes were very useful in training Panchas in issues of social concern, development schemes and programmes. In HP, besides training by the government, there are also programmes run by NGOs to help the villagers, particularly Dalits.

In MP, the Panchas complained that their relationship with the panchayat secretary was not cordial as he did not listen to their requests and complaints and cheated many of them. Caste did not seem to matter as red-tapism was experienced by both Dalit and non-Dalit respondents in their dealings with officials. Relationship with other panchayat officials and workers is much better leading to benefit to the Dalits. In MP, in recent years, a number of NGOs have entered and are working to improve the capabilities of Dalit members of the panchayat. They provide training, hold awareness meetings, provide information about programmes, organize literacy programmes, provide assistance in obtaining help through these programmes, establish Mahila Mandals to help women etc. Dalits are keen that the NGOs should emerge as spokespersons for them and assist them in obtaining education, represent their problems before the government and organize awareness programmes.

In UP, less than half the Dalit respondents held that they were able to gain the cooperation of the BDO and other officials of the block. Thus, problems of implementation are as much due to official apathy as the conservatism of village society. Most of the Dalit respondents pointed out that their relationship with the block officials was neither cordial nor strained, more help is gained from the Gram Sabha, the panchayat and the Pradhan than the BDO and other functionaries. However, all government officials attend the Gram Sabha meetings regularly. Officials, on the other hand, argued that the Dalit leadership is unable to function properly due to lack of education, weak financial position, deprivation of land and lack of any other gainful employment. However, many felt that they were gradually learning to deal with their responsibilities. In Haryana, Dalit leadership faces a two-fold problem: traditional attitudes on the part of the upper castes and an unsympathetic bureaucracy. Here, the upper caste Panchas are able to join hands with the officials and obtain benefits that should have been enjoyed by the Dalits and other weaker sections.

Thus, the comparative analysis provides us with rich insights into the social context in which panchayats function and the problems that the new emerging Dalit leadership faces. It also shows that reservation has proved to be a significant avenue of bringing Dalits into the panchayats and making them members of local governance bodies. This is a historic step as they were earlier excluded, their interests were not taken care of, they received few if any of the fruits of economic development and they could not participate in local politics. The panchayats were captured by the upper castes, who used them to strengthen their own position and corner all benefits meant for the weaker sections and lower castes. Reservations have initiated a process of inclusion of Dalits into the process of local politics and governance providing them a stake in local affairs and decisions regarding development. Panchayats have been made the third tier in the federal structure and provided funds, which makes them more important than in the past. Many of the activities earlier performed by the district or state level bodies have now been handed over to the panchyats.

However, the study also suggests that while reservations can provide Dalits representation in panchayats, it does not ensure that they are able to effectively participate in decision-making and determine local development or obtain benefits that can lead to upliftment of the community. The present study of selected states provides much evidence to the contrary. Despite the granting of reservation there are examples of Dalits having won a seat due to the support of the upper castes thereby undermining the authority and independence of the elected representatives. Equally important is that although Dalits have entered into panchayats in large numbers, there is little evidence of their being able to effectively participate in the decision-making process as equal members. In most cases the non-Dalit participants, due to their better educational attainments, social status, experience and understanding of the process, are able to dominate the proceedings and take decisions, which are in their advantage. With some exceptions, this is even more true in the case of Dalit women who have entered public life very recently. While there are a few Dalit leaders who due to their education and political assertiveness are able to participate, they are often unable to help their community due to lack of organized support in the panchayat.

Panchayats in the states such as HP and UP have introduced a number of developmental programmes, such as building roads, school and panchayat buildings, public bathrooms, improving drainage systems etc., which have benefited both Dalits and non-Dalits. However, little progress has been achieved to solve the specific and distinct problems faced by Dalits, such as removing untouchability and building better houses, access to common village resources, landlessness etc. Despite the existence of governmental programmes to get rid of such problems, they have remained unattended due to the inability of Dalits to fight for such causes. This study also indicates that factional rivalries between sub-castes of Dalits such as between Chamars and Balmikis in UP have come in the way of organized struggle by Dalits to gain a better position within the panchayats. There is little evidence that political parties such as the BSP are able to help Dalits at the village level where upper caste groups confront them. Nor has the state through its bureaucratic apparatus been able to introduce change in the functioning of the panchayat. There is also evidence of the bureaucracy and the upper castes joining hands to the disadvantage of the Dalits. The power structure at the village level remains skewed in favour of the upper castes/classes leaving out the lower and weaker sections.

However, the study does not present a completely negative picture. The importance of reservation in panchayats cannot and should not be underrated. It has been a historic step that has brought a critical mass into these institutions with a potential to question older, traditional, social and political structures and introduce change. This has not yet happened but there is evidence of the beginnings of a social transformation. The very symbolic importance of the introduction of reservation in panchayats must be accepted. It is very different from reservation in parliament or the state legislatures, where the numbers are much larger. On the contrary, at the panchayat level the number of seats are fewer and with the granting of substantial financial powers to these institutions the stakes to hold power are much higher. A long-term process of democratization in the post-independence period is gradually throwing up everywhere a new upwardly mobile, more socially aware and aggressive Dalit generation, which is no longer prepared to put with discrimination and expects a share in the fruits of development. Economic development is also throwing up new avenues and land is no longer the only source of power and prestige. Thus, what we are witnessing is a phase of transition where complete control is no longer in the hands of the upper caste/class elites in the villages but it has not passed into the hands of the Dalits and other weaker sections in the village. The latter have questioned the power of the former but have not been able to remove them. As it is happening in a democratic system, it is taking place gradually and often without our realizing it.

The 73rd Constitutional Amendment Act has aided this process by providing reservation to Dalits and other weaker sections. However, reservations alone cannot carry forward this democratic process. As the study has shown, provisions of education and employment by the state, which will help raise capabilities and awareness among Dalits, together with political mobilization through civil society and political parties, would help carry forward the process. The process of change from aristocratic to democratic politics is going on but remains incomplete.

7

Summing Up

The present study has attempted with the use of empirical data to understand the changing face of PRIs following the passage of the 73rd Constitutional Amendment Act. The passage of this Act is the end product of a long journey in the history of panchayats in the country. Started as local self-governing institutions but with little powers or responsibilities under the colonial state, the introduction of PRIs in post-independence India was a significant step. Leaders such as Mahatma Gandhi pointed out that in a large and diverse country, provision of local self-governing structures would promote democracy. Moreover, traditionally, panchayats had existed in India though their structure and role was different. The question of establishing PRIs had generated much discussion in the Constituent Assembly with members like Dr. B.R. Ambedkar opposing them as traditional institutions, which were undemocratic and oppressive of the weaker sections in the village. However, the Nehruvian State felt that establishing panchayats in a democratic set-up would in time give a blow to the discriminatory caste structure and break the power of the landowning elite by introducing change in village India. Many scholars and administrators were skeptical of this and much literature exists which shows that panchayats were captured by the better off sections of the rural areas and the weaker sections could not participate in them. In short, panchayats were a reflection of a society that in the early years of independence was elitist and undemocratic. A gradual process of democratization of society and polity began but it took time for it to have an impact upon the village and the panchayat institutions within it.

The passing of the 73rd Constitutional Amendment Act in 1992 was a step in keeping with the changes that were taking place in rural India. By the early 1990s, the power of the traditionally higher and middle caste and landowning groups had begun to be questioned though by no means broken by the lower castes and weaker sections within the villages. Political mobilization, particularly in regions such as the Gangetic plains, which had not experienced much social change earlier, rise in social awareness of a new educated and upwardly mobile Dalit leadership and emergence of political parties such as the BSP, introduced change. There was democratization and regionalization of politics due to the social deepening of democracy in a number of states lying in the Hindi heartland whose full impact has yet to be felt. It is these changes that make the new panchayats significant and hold out hope of their democratization. The provision of reservation increased the number of Dalits in the panchayats but such numerical representation itself does not ensure empowerment of weaker sections unless and until it gets transformed into effective participation.

The passage of the 73rd amendment was also the result of the felt need in the polity for decentralization of power and decision-making downwards. The tight federal mould in which the polity was cast, was also needed to be unravelled. The new panchayats have hence been granted much greater powers and responsibilities for local development and funds to make this possible. They have been made a third tier in the federal structure with a distinct constitutional position and role.

Unlike in the past, elections are held in time and the powers and responsibilities of the panchayats have been more clearly defined. The initiation of the structural adjustment programme in 1991 also created the need for greater decentralization and local bodies assuming greater responsibilities. The major promise of democratic decentralization, it was felt, was that it brings popular participation and accountability to local governance and therefore makes it more responsive to the needs and desires of villagers and more effective in delivering services. The revamping of the panchayats has come to be seen as part of the process of reform. Most important for our purposes was that reservations were granted to the Dalits and other weaker sections in order to democratize the functioning of the panchayats and ensure that they do not remain the preserve of the influential in the countryside. It was hoped that with the upsurge from below taking place among the Dalits in parts of the country seminal changes would occur in the traditional power structure of the village and the working of the new panchayats.

The concept of participation is central to the new panchayats. Until the 1970s, it was not part of the literature on policy formulation. But, since then, it has taken on a new meaning. The earlier emphasis on political participation – while giving citizens a right to vote – did not give importance to their capabilities in contributing effectively to the designing of public policy that was seen as something done by administrators and experts. But, in more recent years, there has been a demand from the grassroots for inclusion into this field, which has broadened the concept giving citizens a greater say and political space to develop their own needs and voices. Today, this demand is emerging from the disadvantaged groups, who feel they have not been adequately represented so far in the making of policy and in fruits of economic development. With the current preoccupation with decentralization and democratization and simultaneously the introduction of reservations in the new panchayats, the meaning, nature and scope of participation of weaker sections has widened. Participation today does not mean mere use of government benefits but being part of the state-delivered programmes.

A second concept is that of accountability. Public accountability means that elected representatives are responsible to citizens for the performance of their duties and this is an important feature of democratic governance. At the level of the panchayats this means that the Panchas are responsible to all the villagers for the work they undertake for development on their behalf. An additional aspect is that Dalit Panchas owe a special responsibility to their community as they are expected to look after their specific needs and interests in the panchayats. It is questionable how far these ideas have assumed importance in the working of the new panchayats.

Against this backdrop, the present study examined the usefulness of reservation of seats for Dalits and also Dalit women in the new panchayats in four states. A central question examined through fieldwork was whether reservation has been able to work as a means of introducing social change whereby Dalits can function as equal members. While reservation was provided in a few states such as Karnataka earlier but it was for a short period and did not have constitutional sanction. More specifically, the goal of the study was two-fold: to provide a profile of the new emerging Dalit leadership among the Sarpanchas and Panchas and, second, to understand how far they have been able to participate in the actual functioning and particularly in the decision-making processes in the panchayats. Democratization has thrown up an educated and socially conscious new generation of Dalit leaders in a number of states. Earlier, social status, landownership, economic power and political influence enabled the traditional elite to control the working of the panchayats. A major question is whether the new Dalit leadership has made a dent in the traditional power structure within the village, which excluded them from the working of the panchayats. An attempt was also made to identify the factors, which have helped or hindered effective and meaningful functioning by these leaders.

The study shows that reservations have been accepted and Dalits have entered into the new panchayats. They have been supported in elections not only by their own community but also in many cases by villagers belonging to other castes. Thus, they have managed to gain ground in local governance institutions from which they were largely deprived of in the past. This has been possible due to changing social attitudes and improvement in the position of Dalits. Dalit women have also gained acceptance and support within the panchayats and among the villagers. This is a positive step as Dalits have rarely been members of panchayats or Sarpanchas earlier. However, while Dalits have managed to enter the new panchayats, this has not led to effective participation or a share in the benefits that panchayats provide. The study found that elected representatives were not able to articulate group-specific interests or exercise their own judgement in decision-making. Dalits do not take part in the deliberations or contribute to major decisions, which determine local governance and development. While in some cases Dalits have been able to make their presence felt, in most states, this is a shift that has yet to take place. A number of the Dalit representatives were answerable to the elites of the village and remained under their control rather than showing any accountability to the villagers. Panchayats are not yet democratic institutions nor are they arenas of contestation and debate.

The study further shows that there are marked differences in the manner in which panchayats function in the four selected states. All-India generalizations are not of much use in understanding the manner in which panchayats function. As in the case of all democratic institutions, they are embedded in and therefore determined to a large extent by the social, economic and political context in which they are placed and function. The differences among the states arise out of the pace at which the process of socio-economic change and development is taking place within them. In our study education, economic independence and political consciousness emerge as determining factors that enable Dalits to make full use of the chance that reservation has provided them to participate in the new panchayats. Education can provide them the self-confidence, knowledge and awareness of the functioning of the panchayats and the ability to take part in deliberations and decision-making. HP provides a good example of a state where literacy rates are high and Dalits have with confidence entered into the new panchayats. In contrast, in states such as UP and MP, Dalit leaders lack basic information about the panchayats and the capability to participate in the process of governance.

Second, in the states where a more inclusive pattern of economic development has helped Dalits to improve their economic status, it has provided them the potential to revolt against the traditional order and at least initiate a process of reordering relationships within the panchayats. Traditionally, Dalits have owned little land and have depended upon the landowning class in the village to provide them employment leading to a culture of dependency. This inhibited them from participating in the panchayats. Again, HP is a good example where the state has not only helped in raising literacy among Dalits but also helped them through subsidies to take up horticulture and improve their economic condition. However, the study also clearly indicates that while education and economic betterment are important, unless the conservative social structure, which has traditionally oppressed and suppressed Dalits, undergoes a change, not much can be achieved in the new panchayats. In recent years, social and political awareness among Dalits has led them to question the traditional unequal caste structure and demand more egalitarian institutional structures, which provide them space to participate and a share in decision-making. In some states this process has made a beginning and its impact upon the functioning of panchayats is beginning to be felt. As the study reveals, it is not merely caste *per se* that is the major obstacle for Dalits today, rather it is competition to control common property resources in the village and the benefits from panchayats between various social groups. Ritual untouchability has been largely replaced by caste-based competition; upper caste groups use their social position to corner benefits provided by the state or to prevent Dalits from becoming powerful and questioning their position. Thus, a major conclusion of our analysis is that reservations alone cannot provide empowerment unless Dalits also have the wealth to make use of it.

The significance of these factors is even more clearly visible in the case of Dalit women. Traditionally, Dalit women have suffered on account of both caste and gender and while they have been part of the workforce, they have not played any role in the panchayats. The study suggests that in states where the rate of literacy and the status of women remain low, providing Dalit women reservation has not led to their active participation. They remain proxies of their husbands or other male relatives. In HP where traditionally the status of women was better than in the northern plains, the sex ratio is more favourable and literacy rates have risen in recent years, they enjoy a better status in the panchayats than in the other states studied. While they are not yet part of the decision-making process, they freely attend meetings and voice their opinions. A sharp contrast is Haryana, which remains feudal and patriarchal and women do not enjoy any voice in local governance. In MP and UP, Dalit women are in a similar situation but rise of social consciousness and the emergence of woman Chief Minister such as Mayawati have been important symbols of change.

Another significant aspect, which emerged in the study is the role that NGOs have come to play in rural development. With the retreat of the state from many welfare activities NGOs have become important. They are active in helping Dalits and other disadvantaged groups to understand the functioning of the new panchayats and their role in improving the lives of villagers. A partnership has emerged between the government and NGOs in many areas such as education, public health, training in panchayats and infrastructural development etc. This role is bound to increase in the future affecting the role that panchayats play in the rural areas.

All this brings into question the very notion of representation of marginalized groups through reservations. Reservations have ensured election of Dalits to the new panchayats. But these have not ensured the effective representation of disadvantaged groups in the panchayats with respect to participation of elected members, their responsiveness to villagers' needs and interest and accountability to the local government. However, there are undoubtedly signs of change in all the states under the present study. Dalits have realized the importance of panchayats and are making efforts to improve their position within these institutions. What is required is a concerted effort on the part of the state to improve the educational attainments, economic position and understanding of the functioning of local government on the part of Dalits so that they are able to participate as equal citizens.

In order to make the constitutional provisions effective in terms of encouraging Dalits and women to participate actively in politics, it is imperative for the government to facilitate them with infrastructure inputs of the state apparatus so that they could be effective. Following measures could be extremely useful in this regard:

1. *Not mere politicization but also political socialization*: It is not mere politicization but political socialization which could help Dalits realize their actual role as effective leaders in the panchayats. Besides non-Dalit leaders and Panchas had their own likes and dislikes which restrict their interaction with others. The political socialization is also needed to ensure communicative interaction with members of other castes and male members of women leaders.

2. *Transforming role perception of leaders*: The role perception of Dalit leaders need to be changed. It was felt that with their representation in local bodies they have got an

opportunity to favour some of their own people by way of constructing *pucca* roads, build drainage, upgrade schools, and involve themselves in many activities of rural development. Very soon, they realized that to be effective in implementing those decisions, they required a great deal of persuasive efforts in the block offices backed up by repeated official communications, and this was the role that they had never visualized. Their visualizing political role in carrying out the development activities is contingent upon several other factors which they need to understand.

3. *Imparting functional education and training*: There is need to impart functional knowledge and training to the Panchas holding office in the local bodies. As a matter of fact vast majority of the Panchas were just literate and that posed a major handicap in their way to be distinguished as an effective leader. There had been difference in the levels of education among the states. It needs to be emphasized that as most of the official communications and procedures are complicated so they need to get special training. In order to make them effective, they need to have minimum knowledge to understand the working styles of office. For women leaders, lack of functional education has made them to depend more on their menfolk.

There is also need to provide legal and technical knowledge for the effective functioning of the leaders represented in the local bodies. The members, specially belonging to Dalit sections and women, lack education and have no knowledge about the legal and technical matters. Even if, they have some understanding of these matters, it is about its operational aspects and its nature is highly restrictive. And, therefore, it becomes imperative on the part of the government to facilitate Dalit leaders with all the required legal and technical information so that they understand the importance of the functioning and their roles as a leader in the local bodies. It is only when they visualize their roles in the local bodies that they could effectively participate in its functioning.

4. *Celebrating days of importance and initiating positive discourse on social issues*: Apart from celebrating Independence Day or Republican Day, the panchayat leaders also need to celebrate the days commemorating the social reformers like Mahatma Phuley, Periyar, Dr. Ambedkar etc. as symbolic gesture where ensuring community participation of the village folks could remove the caste barriers and reservations that the people have about the Dalits. The Dalit leaders could also take initiative in organizing certain cultural activities of the members belonging to Dalits in particular and village folks in general so as to make Dalit leaders feel integrated with the village community.

It was also noticed that the Dalit leaders had least inclination to discuss issues relating to women's health, children's health, dowry, corruption, female foeticide, youth unemployment, women's education, prohibition, environmental pollution, family planning etc. It was somewhat regrettable to note that the leaders did not visualize any role on these matters, which could change the life of the village folks and, therefore, the leaders failed to initiate a positive discourse on social issues mentioned above.

5. *Role of civil society initiatives*: The problem of Dalits is concerned primarily with social dimensions and thus it needs social solutions. If it would have been lack of economic power only, then perhaps, the recent incident of caste violence in Gohana of Haryana State would not have occurred. The Dalit residents of the locality which was set on fire had been quite independent of feudal crutches so not only economically independent but also having some sort of economic affluency. If such is the situation, then civil society initiatives where not only Dalits but also non-Dalits take active participation become imperative. Though, some NGOs have been working in the blocks of MP, but their role has been negligible. And, in rest of the blocks, the initiatives by sincere NGOs need to be taken so that a beginning of civil society initiatives could be made.

Bibliography

Adiseshiah, 1964. *Social Background and Role Preference of Village Pradhans*, New Delhi, Institute of Social Dalitiences, New Delhi.

Ali, Sadiq, 1964. Report of the Study Team on Panchayati Raj, Jaipur, Government of Rajasthan.

Ashok Mehta Committee, 1978. Report of the Committee on Panchayati Raj Institutions, Government of India, Ministry of Agriculture and Irrigation, Department of Rural Development.

Aziz, A., 2000. "Democratic Decentralisation: Experience of Karnataka", *Economic and Political Weekly,* Vol. XXXV, No. 39, September: 23-39.

Balwantrai Mehta, 1957. Report of the Committee on Panchayati Raj Institutions, Government of India.

Beteille, Andre, 1974. *Studies in Agrarian Social Structure*, New Delhi: Oxford University Press.

Buch, N. Jain and S.N. Chaudhary, 1999. Women in Panchayati Raj in Madhya Pradesh (Mimeo), Mahila Chetna Manch, Bhopal.

Census of India, 2001. Office of the Registrar General of India, *Compact Disc.*

Chakraborty, Krishna and Swapan K. Bhattacharyya 1993. *Leadership Factions and PR: A Case Study of West Bengal*, Jaipur and New Delhi: Rawat Publications.

Crook, Richard C. and James Manor, 1998. *Democracy and Decentralisation in South Asia and West Africa Participation, Accountability and Performance*, UK: Oxford University Press.

Desai, Vasant, 1990. *Panchayati Raj*, New Delhi: Himalaya.

Dreze, Jean and Harris Gazdar, 1997. "U.P.: The Burden of Inertia" in Jean Dreze and Amartya Sen (eds.), *Indian Development: Selected Regional Perspectives*, Oxford University Press: 31-128.

Guhan, S. 1995. "Centre and States in the Reform Process in India." In Robert Cassen and Vijay Joshi (eds.), *The Future of Reform*, 73-111: Oxford University Press.

Gulati, Chandrika, 2000. "Panchayati Raj in India: Problems and Prospects." In Satu Kahkonen and Anthony Lanyi (eds.), *Institutions, Incentives and Economic Reform in India*, New Delhi: Sage Publications, 367-411.

Gurumurthy, U., 1987. *Panchayati Raj and the Weaker Sections*, New Delhi: Ashish Publishing House.

Hirway, I., 1986. "Panchayati Raj at the Crossroads", *Economic and Political Weekly*, July 22: 1663-1667.

Jha, S.N. and P.C. Mathur (eds.), 1999. *Decentralisation and Local Politics Readings in Indian Government and Politics-2*, New Delhi: Sage Publications.

Journal of Political Economy XII, Nos. 3 and 4, 2000. Special issue on Scheduled Castes in India, July-December.

Kaushik, Susheela, 1995. *Panchayati Raj in Action: Challenges to Women's Role*, New Delhi: Friedrich Ebert Stifting.

Khanna, B.S., 1994. *Panchayati Raj: Rural Local Self-government National Perspectives and State Studies in India*, New Delhi: Deep and Deep.

Lele, M.K., 2001. "Local Government: Conflict of Interests and Issues of Legitimization", *Economic and Political Weekly*, Vol. XXXVI, No. 51, December 22-28.

Lieten, G.K. and Ravi Srivastava, 1999. *Unequal Partners Power Relations, Devolution and Development in Uttar Pradesh Indo-Dutch Studies on Development Alternatives*-23, New Delhi: Sage.

Mahipal, 1998. "Women in Panchayats: Experiences of a Training Camp," *Economic and Political Weekly*, Vol. XXIII, No. 4, January 24-30: 150-52.

— 2002. "Panchayats in Fifth Scheduled Areas," *Economic and Political Weekly*, Vol. XXXV, No. 19, May 6-12, p. 1602.

Majumdar, A.K. and Bhanwar Singh (eds.), 1997. *Historical and Conceptual Development of Panchayati Raj*, New Delhi: Radha Publications.

Mansbridge, Jane, 2000. "What Does a Representative Do? DeDalitriptive Representation in Communicative Settings of Distrust, Uncrystallised Interests, and Historically Denigrated Status," in Will Kymlicka and Wayne Norman (eds.), *Citizenship in Diverse Societies*, New Delhi: Oxford University Press, 99-174.

Mathew, George, 2004. "Local Self Government and Dalits" in Bibek Debroy and D. Shyam Babu (eds.), *The Dalit Question Reforms and Social Justice,* Globus Books with Rajiv Gandhi Institute for Contemporary Studies, New Delhi: 255-262.

Mathew, George and Ramesh C. Nayak, 1996. "Panchayats at Work What it Means for the Oppressed?" *Economic and Political Weekly*, Vol. XXXI, No. 27, July 6: 1765-1771.

Mathur, M.V. and Narain, Iqbal, 1969. *Panchayati Raj Planning and Democracy*, Bombay: Asia Publishing House.

Mehta, B.R. Committee Report, 1957. Report of the Team for the Study of Community Projects and National Extension Services, New Delhi.

Mendelsohn, Oliver, 1993. "The Transformation of Authority in Rural India" *Modern Asian Studies,* Vol. 27, No. 4: 804-42.

Mishra, S.N. and S.S. Singh, 1993. *Roads to Model Panchayati Raj*, New Delhi: Mittal Publications.

Mishra, S.N., 1997. *Poverty Alleviation Programs and Gram Panchayats*, New Delhi: Mittal.

Mitra, Subrata K. and Chiriyankandath James, 1992. *Electoral Politics in India: A Changing Landscape*, New Delhi: Segments Books.

Mittal, S.C., 1986. *Haryana: A Historical Perspective*, New Delhi: Atlantic Publishers and Distributors.

Mohapatra, Ajaya Kumar, 2002, *State of Panchayats in Himachal Pradesh*, PRIA, New Delhi.

Murthy, O.K., 1969. Some Reflections on the Duplication of Panchayati Raj on the Weaker Sections of the Community, in the Proceedings of the 15th Conferences of the K.S. Co.

Narender Kumar, 1999. *Scheduled Castes and Panchayat Elections in Haryana*, New Delhi: Indian Social Institute.

— 2004. *Dalit Policies, Politics and Parliament*, Delhi: Shipra.

Pai, Sudha, 2000. "Pradhanis in the New Panchayats: A Study from Meerut District" in Kiran Saxena (ed.), *Women and Politics*, New Delhi: Gyan Publishing House.

Pai, Sudha, 2002. *Dalit Assertion and the Unfinished Democratic Revolution*, New Delhi: Sage.

Palanithurai, G. (ed.), 1996, *Empowering People*, New Delhi: Kanishka.

—, 1995. *People Perception of Politics: An Indian Perspective*, Delhi: Kanishka Publishers and Distributors.

Papola, T.S., 1989. "Uttar Pradesh" in M. Adiseshiah (ed.), *Economic of the States of The Indian Union*, New Delhi: Lancer International: 63-70.

— 2000. "Dalit Assertion in Tamil Nadu: An Exploratory Note", *Journal of Indian School of Political Economy*, Vol. XII, Nos. 3 and 4, July – December: 501-18.

Parvathamma, 1975. "Panchayat Raj and the Weaker Sections", unpublished paper presented at the Seminar on Panchayats and Weaker Sections, NIRD, 1975, Hyderabad.

Patnaik, Pratyusna, 2005. "Affirmative Action and Representation of Weaker Sections Participation and Accountability in Orissa's Panchayats", *Economic and Political Weekly,* October 29: 4753-61.

Pundir, J.K. 1995. "Development of Dalitheduled Castes: A Study of their Political and Decisive Participation at Local Level in Rural Areas" *AJSDJ* Vol. III: 49-64.

Pushpendra, 1999. "Dalit Assertion through Electoral Politics" *Economic and Political Weekly,* Vol. XXXIV, No. 36, September 4: 2609-2618.

Shankar, Kripa, 1998. "Agricultural Labours in East UP", *Economic and Political Weekly*, 12 June: 1211-14.

Shariff, Abusaleh, 1999. *Profile of the Indian States*, NCAER report, New Delhi: Oxford University Press.

Sheshadri and S. Azim, 2001. "Evaluation of Decentralised Governance and Planning in Karnataka" *Man and Development*, June.

Shiviah, M. et al., 1980. *Panchayat Raj Elections in West Bengal 1978: A Study in Institution Building for Rural Development*, Hyderabad: National Institute of Rural Development.

Shymala, C.K., 2001. "Elected Representatives in Rural Decentralised Governance: Socio-economic Analysis of Zilla Panchayat Members of Karnataka", *Man and Development,* June.

Singh, D.R., 1985. *Rural Leadership Among Dalitheduled Castes*, Allahabad: Chugh Publications.

Singh, Soran, 1987. *Scheduled Castes of India: Dimensions of Social Change*, Delhi: Gian Publishing House.

Srinivas, M.N., 1966. *Social Change in Modern India*, Berkeley: University of California Press.

Varshney, Ashutosh, *India and the Politics of Developing Countries: Essays in Memory of Myron Weiner*, New Delhi: Sage Publications.

Wood, Evelyn, 1959. "Patterns of Influence within Rural India", in Park, R.L. and Tinker, I. (eds.), *Leadership and Political Institutions in India*, Princeton: Princeton University Press.

Yadav, J.S., Factionalism in Haryana Village, *American Anthropologist*, Vol. 70, No. 5, 1968, pp. 909-11.

Index